This Book Belongs to:

Jalen
Khendall
Bryce
Dunlap

FAMILY BIBLE STORY

# ADAM & EVE

Presented to

...................................................................................................

by

...................................................................................................

on this date

...................................................................................................

To order, call

**1-800-765-6955**

or go to

www.familybiblestory.com

For information on other Review and Herald® products

visit us at

www.reviewandherald.com

# FAMILY BIBLE STORY

# ADAM&EVE

*Text by*
## RUTH REDDING BRAND

*Color paintings by* Raoul Vitale
*Pencil illustrations by* Darrel Tank

REVIEW AND HERALD® PUBLISHING ASSOCIATION
HAGERSTOWN, MD 21740

Pencil Illustrations Copyright © 2005 by Darrel Tank. All Rights Reserved under the Pan-American and International Copyright Conventions.

Scriptures credited to ICB are quoted from the *International Children's Bible, New Century Version,* copyright © 1983, 1986, 1988 by Word Publishing, Dallas, Texas 75039. Used by permission.

Bible texts credited to NRSV are from the New Revised Standard Version of the Bible, copyright © 1989 by the Division of Christian Education of the National Council of the Churches of Christ in the U.S.A. Used by permission.

This book was

Edited by Richard W. Coffen

Copyedited by Jocelyn Fay, Delma Miller, and James Cavil

Designed by Trent Truman

Cover art by Raoul Vitale

Typeset: Galliard 13/22

PRINTED IN U.S.A.

08  07  06  05          5  4  3  2  1

**R&H Cataloging Service**

Family Bible Story

   V. Adam and Eve

  1. Bible Stories.  I. Brand, Ruth Redding

    220.9505

ISBN 0-8280-1850-2 hardcover

ISBN 0-8280-1851-0 paperback

# DEDICATED TO

*Gail Hunt—*

artist, designer, musician,
dreamer, genius, and

the inspiration for this book.

# CONTENTS

# WHY THESE BOOKS?

*"Duty, faith, love, are roots, and ever green."*—GEORGE PEELE, *"A Farewell to Arms"*

It does not bode well when a civilization disconnects from its spiritual roots. And the evidence suggests that Western culture is losing its spiritual legacy. Daily newspapers, the evening news broadcasts, and the content of many Web sites seem to make the compelling case that popular culture has become disconnected from its spiritual underpinnings. It's time for us to reconnect with our spiritual heritage.

Enter the *Family Bible Story* series.

First, notice the overall title of the series. Emphasis is on the *Bible*, the sacred text of two of the world's religions. Other major world religions have their own sacred texts, but the producers of the *Family Bible Story* know little about those other traditions. However, we *do* know something about the Bible and want to share it with you.

Second, the emphasis here is on *story*. The Judeo-Christian Scripture contains genealogies, songs, sermons, letters, prophecies, apocalypses, as well as stories. This set of books concentrates on the narratives. Good stories well told have great power to captivate the imagination, inculcate traditional values, and enhance character development. We've focused on some of the grandest morality-building stories found in Scripture.

Third, the series is for the *family*. We want this set of books to serve the needs of the entire family—not just wriggly preschoolers, not just grade school kids, not just inquisitive adults. So each unit has something to offer the entire family. Even seasoned Bible students will learn something new in this series.

The key word to describe the *Family Bible Story* is "realism." Our goal has been to achieve literary

**OPENING BLACK-&-WHITE DRAWING**
Every story will open with a delightful little black-and-white pencil drawing by Darrel Tank.

**THE BIBLE STORIES**
These Bible stories for school-age children were especially written for this new series by Ruth Redding Brand. The stories are all written at a fifth-grade reading level and are designed to be read by children ages 9 through 12.

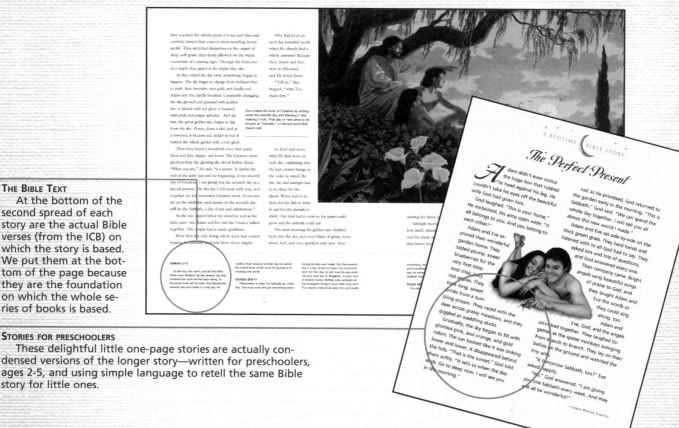

**THE BIBLE TEXT**

At the bottom of the second spread of each story are the actual Bible verses (from the ICB) on which the story is based. We put them at the bottom of the page because they are the foundation on which the whole series of books is based.

**STORIES FOR PRESCHOOLERS**

These delightful little one-page stories are actually condensed versions of the longer story—written for preschoolers, ages 2-5, and using simple language to retell the same Bible story for little ones.

virtual reality. Each component has been included to help achieve that effect. Let's examine each element and the rationale for including it.

At the base of the second spread of each chapter are the *Bible verses* that tell the original story. The Scriptures constitute the very foundation of all that we want to accomplish in the *Family Bible Story*. Often we've had to shorten the biblical account because of space limitations. Nevertheless, the retelling of these stories is closely tied to the original biblical account.

We chose the *International Children's Bible* (ICB) because of its clarity. It's difficult to misunderstand the ICB. The vocabulary is simple. Ideas are crystal clear. It's "the only version that [can] be comprehended on a third-grade instructional level." The translators also focused on being "accurate and faithful to the original manuscripts." Its contemporary, easy-to-read language contributes to

the overall realism we seek.

A *time line* is included in most of the books. It's important to know how a particular story fits into the overall time scheme within the biblical world as well as within the rest of the world. These historical time lines help pinpoint the time period in which these stories unfolded.

Each *full-length story* has been carefully crafted to maintain the effect of realism. Author Ruth Brand, a teacher of composition, spent nearly eight years crafting the stories found in this set.

Personal descriptions of the actors, creative characterization, carefully crafted dialogue, attention to plot development, delineation of background settings, utilization of ancient Near Eastern customs, compliance with the original biblical text—all these build realism.

Each story is written at a fifth-grade readability level. Vocabulary has been controlled, while sentence structure has been varied. We felt we could reach the most children that way.

A chief concern has been the picture of God. Does God come across as a real person, or a shadowy nobody? The author has tried to portray a loving being who created us with the gift of free will and who cares deeply about us. Indeed, He cares enough that on occasion He enters the story as one of the major characters. He's a God with emotions, a God with intellect, a God who models compassion—even when He is said to be angry. He is, above all, the God who "so loved the world, that he gave . . ." (John 3:16).

Each story is lavishly illustrated with new *artwork*, and sometimes with *photographs* and *maps*. Specially commissioned artists have prepared original illustrations for the *Family Bible Story*. Popular depictions of Bible stories in much of contemporary literature tend to be cartoonish. We believe that cartoons have their place. However, we feel that cartoons of Bible characters often tend to destroy realism, not enhance it.

The photographs of biblical places and objects have been carefully chosen. Ur was a real city. The Dead Sea still exists. By including photographs of the geographical locales—and archaeological artifacts, as well—we enhance the realism of the stories.

Occasionally we've added maps that have been prepared from scratch by the publisher. They help put biblical places in relationship to each other. If a story involves movement of the characters, we've tried to show that as clearly as possible on the maps.

Most drawings, photographs, and maps are accompanied by *captions*. We've tried to write them in such a way that they don't merely repeat information found in the stories but provide additional content.

Some stories feature a *Did You Know?* box.

These short essays are written for adolescents and adults who want to know more about the technical side of the ancient Near Eastern world. This information has been culled from the findings of the best biblical researchers around the world.

Finally, each story ends with a *Bedtime Bible Story*—the same story written in a style specifically adapted for preschoolers. After all, if we want the children of the world to know the great stories of Scripture, we should begin when they are babies. These Bedtime Bible Stories are short and adapted so as not to frighten little children. (They should be able to fall asleep afterward.) Nonetheless, they outline the details of the main story in such a way that little tots can grasp them. Even a small child can learn to trust in God.

Each volume ends with a *glossary* that offers information about every biblical person and place mentioned in the book. But how does one pronounce those ancient tongue twisters? Some dictionaries today give popular English-language pronunciations of these names, but we thought that wasn't enough. So we asked a biblical linguist, Leona Glidden Running, to explain how those names were pronounced in ancient Egypt, Babylon, or Canaan.

We believe that the traditional values of our Judeo-Christian legacy can still provide a safe harbor for children growing up in contemporary culture. It is our hope that these *Family Bible Story* books will make Scripture come alive for you and for your entire family. We pray that your children will delight in the truths that formed our faith and made us strong, and come to know heaven's richest blessing.

May all who drink at these fountains rise to greet the day with gladness and fall asleep in the peace of God.

—THE PUBLISHERS

| FIRST DAY | SECOND DAY | THIRD DAY | FOURTH DAY | FIFTH DAY | SIXTH DAY | SEVENTH DAY |
|---|---|---|---|---|---|---|
| Evening/Morning | Evening/Morning | Evening/Morning | Evening/Morning | Evening/Morning | Evening/Morning | Evening/Morning |

"Let there be light . . . God called the light Day, and the darkness he called Night" (Genesis 1:3-5).

"Let there be a firmament. . . . God called the firmament Heaven" (Genesis 1:6-8).

"Let the dry land appear. . . . Let the earth bring forth grass, the herb, . . . and the . . . tree" (Genesis 1:9-11).

"Let there be lights in the firmament. . . . The greater light to rule the day, and the lesser light to rule the night: he made the stars also" (Genesis 1:14-16).

"Let the waters bring forth abundantly. . . . and fowl that may fly above the earth" (Genesis 1:20).

"Let the earth bring forth . . . cattle, and creeping thing, and beast. . . . Let us make man in our image" (Genesis 1:24-26).

"[God] rested on the seventh day. . . . God blessed the seventh day, and sanctified it" (Genesis 2:2, 3).

## ADAM

Adam was the first person created by God. The Hebrew word—even in the Genesis Creation story—has three meanings: (a) human beings in a generic sense; (b) the first male *Homo sapiens;* and (c) Adam, the name of the first man. After he and Eve sinned God made them leave the Garden of Eden. Adam, Scripture tells us, lived for 930 years.

## EVE

Eve, the first woman God created, was Adam's wife. According to the Genesis account of Creation, God made Eve from one of Adam's ribs. Adam first named her *Ishshah,* "woman," but after she was tempted by a serpent in the Garden of Eden (the Fall) he renamed her Eve. The Bible says that she was a "helper fit for" Adam.

## ENOCH

The name Enoch means "dedicated one." He was the "seventh from Adam" and is said to have "walked with God" after his wife gave birth to their son Methuselah. Scholars are not sure how to understand the Hebrew behind the expression "walked with God." When Enoch was 365 years old, God translated him—took him alive to heaven.

## NOAH

God asked Noah to build an ark. He obeyed and built a boat 450 feet long, 75 feet wide, and 45 feet high. Noah, through his sons and daughters-in-law, became the progenitor of the human race. He is the first person to plant a vineyard after the Flood. Noah died when he was 950 years old. He's the first person on record to get drunk.

"In the beginning God created the heaven and the earth."

*Genesis 1:1*

# A BRAND-NEW PLANET

Where is the darkest place you have ever been? Perhaps it was your house when the lights went out because of a storm. On a moonless night, before anyone found the candles or a flashlight, it was dark, wasn't it? Now think about the darkest place you can even imagine. What about the bottom of a coal mine at midnight, with someone holding black velvet gloved hands over your eyes?

Before God made this world, it was even darker.

What is the most water you have ever seen? The Mississippi River? Lake Superior? The Atlantic or Pacific Ocean, which seem never to end? But every river has another side; lakes have shorelines; even the vast oceans wash up thousands of miles on the other side of the world.

Before God made this world, water covered everything. A shoreless deep ocean rolled around a coal-black planet. Nothing more.

Then God stepped into the blackness and the nothingness . . . and spoke. At the sound of His voice, dazzling light drove back the darkness.

The second day God spoke, and blue sky, life-giving air, wrapped around the spinning planet like a soft blanket.

Up from the waters and through the shining mists hills pushed their tops, and on the

third day valleys stretched themselves before their Creator. He spoke, and the hills and valleys shone with a living green. Tall trees swayed in the breeze. Flowers suddenly danced in the valleys and pranced up the hillsides.

On the fourth day the Creator spoke, and the empty sky blazed with that enormous ball we call the sun. As darkness fell, the smaller shining ball we call the moon floated across the inky sky, and billions of stars and galaxies twinkled through space.

At the voice of God the mists vanished, and lakes, ponds, rivers, and seas shimmered in the sunshine. At His command on the fifth day playful orcas and ponderous blue whales and neon tetras and rainbow trout churned the rivers and lakes and seas as they swam. At another word mockingbirds and hummingbirds, eagles and toucans, filled the air with music and color and the whisper of their wings.

Then, at God's command the next day, in a vacant valley, a flock of sheep suddenly grazed, while frogs croaked from a nearby pond and elephants trumpeted a triumphant note. On the hilltops, goats leaped and climbed, while lions and leopards, cows and cats, dogs, deer, rabbits, and thousands of other animals frolicked in the wonderful new world.

God looked around and smiled. But He had not finished yet. The world was beautiful. Everything in it was perfect, but He hadn't created it just for Himself. He had in mind a wonderful creature who would be very much like Himself. So God knelt down on the ground, and as you might work with modeling clay, His strong fingers shaped the claylike dirt.

Carefully, lovingly, He worked. He pulled the clay and stretched it. His fingertips pinched a little here, shaped more carefully there. At last a human form lay on the ground—as though asleep it lay in the dust like a life-size doll.

Then God bent over the quiet face. God opened His mouth and breathed ever so gently into the mouth of the newly formed person. The man's eyelids fluttered, and he opened his eyes.

God smiled.

"Welcome to Eden," He said.

We call that first person "Adam." Adam looked in wonder around him. A brand-new being in a brand-new world, his heart beat with love for the God who had created him and this life-filled planet.

God showed Adam a special place that He had created with him in mind. It was breathtakingly beautiful, a garden park in which Adam would make his home. Then, as the animals walked before him, Adam's quick mind named them one after another. He chuckled at the monkeys. He smiled at the long, long neck of the giraffe. With pleasure he ran his fingers through the thick mane of the lion. But

## THE MAN'S EYELIDS FLUTTERED, AND HE OPENED HIS EYES. GOD SMILED. "WELCOME TO EDEN," HE SAID.

The Bible tells us that God is the Creator of all that is. It also assures us that He is the sustainer of the universe, being constantly active in maintaining it.

after seeing all the animals, Adam felt lonely. All the animals had mates. He had none.

Then God put Adam into a deep sleep. From Adam's side He removed one rib. Taking the rib, He carefully built another creature. It was like Adam, yet not like him, because the lines of its body were softer and more graceful. The shoulders were not as broad, nor was it as tall. Its face was as noble

as Adam's, but more delicate. Then God gently woke Adam and presented him with this beautiful surprise, the last and loveliest of creation—a woman!

Adam smiled and held out his hands as she slipped her hands into his. The first man and the first woman loved each other. They became husband and wife, Adam and Eve.

It had taken just six days for God to complete

God said, "Let the earth be filled with animals. . . . Let there be tame animals and small crawling animals and wild animals. . . ." And it happened. . . .

Then God said, "Let us make human beings in our image and likeness. . . ."

Evening passed, and morning came. This was the sixth day. . . . The Lord God took dust from the ground and formed man from it. The Lord breathed the breath of life into the man's nose. And the man became a living person. . . .

Then the Lord God said, "It is not good for the man to be alone. I will make a helper who is right for him." . . .

God caused the man to sleep very deeply. . . . God took one of the ribs from the man's body. . . . God used the rib . . . to make a woman. Then the Lord brought the woman to the man

# ANCIENT NEAR EASTERN CREATION STORIES

Besides the biblical account in Genesis, the Mesopotamians and the Egyptians had their own explanations of how the world and life began.

The most famous Mesopotamian Creation story is Enuma elish. It tells how two primordial gods, Apsu and Tiamat, created all the other gods. In time the younger deities became rebellious, so Apsu and Tiamat tried to destroy them. Eventually Tiamat created monsters that threatened the younger gods.

Marduk, one of the younger gods, offered to defend his fellow deities if they made him king. They accepted his proposal. After a mighty struggle Marduk killed Tiamat, cutting her in half to make the heavens and the earth.

From the blood of Kingu, another monster that Tiamat had made, Ea, another god, created human beings. Humanity would do the hard work that the lesser gods had previously performed.

In contrast, Genesis tells how God created human beings not to be His servants, but to be stewards of the earth (Genesis 1:26). Nor did He have to battle the forces of chaos. He effortlessly created everything, speaking it into existence.

This Creation story was read annually on the fourth day of the New Year Festival in Babylon.

Egypt had a number of Creation stories. As in the Mesopotamian myths, the first gods spontaneously came into being from natural forces. They then created the other gods. One god, Atum, created everything from his semen. Another god fashioned human beings on a potter's wheel.

The god Ptah, like the God of Genesis, brought everything into existence by speaking. In the beginning the universe was a water-filled chaos. At his command, the waters above separated from the waters below. He spoke dry land into existence, then animals, and finally human beings.

In a way, Ptah was not so much creating something through his own ability as he was employing forces already inherent in the structure of the universe.

The Bible, however, portrays God creating through His own personal power. He Himself established all the natural laws and powers.

Although Scripture might not give us the scientific details that we would like, it does correct the pagan ideas of Creation, assuring us that the Creator cares for and sustains the universe and its living things.

in the beautiful new world. Adam and Eve had never seen the black, lifeless planet just six days earlier, but somehow they knew that God was a worker of miracles, and they worshipped Him.

Have you ever wondered how we know what happened so long ago? Of course, Adam and Eve could tell their own story about Creation, but how do we know what happened before they were created? Over the many years people in Babylon, Canaan, and elsewhere have told all kinds of stories about how the world began.

One day God said, "People have forgotten that I am the only God. They have forgotten that I made the world for them because I love them. They have forgotten that I was there in the beginning, before anything else. I must tell them how I created the world!"

So God chose a man called Moses, a man who came to love Him. God told him to write down the Creation story so that people could read it and not forget it. We can read that story today in our Bibles.

His work. The seventh day of Creation He proclaimed a holy day. On this special day God stayed close to Adam and Eve, and they sat at the feet of their Creator. God gave a low, happy laugh as He looked at Adam and Eve and all the new creatures

# A Brand-new Planet

Let's get started!" God said joyfully.

And the first thing He created was light. "Let there be light!" God said. And sparkling light appeared. God smiled.

On the second day God wrapped a blanket of sweet air all around the earth.

On the third day God looked at the water that covered the earth. "Let the waters be gathered together in one place!" God called out. "Let dry land appear!" And it happened just as He commanded. The waters moved into big seas and lakes. And naked, brown hills and valleys arose.

"Grass!" God exclaimed. "We need tall, swaying grass. And flowers!" He said to Himself. "Pink roses. Purple pansies. Orange poppies." God created all kinds of flowers.

"Now trees!" God decided. "Apple trees! Lemon trees! Giant redwood trees! Slender aspens!"

At the end of the third day God looked around at all He had done. It was good, and God was happy.

On the fourth day God made the great sun to shine on the earth and warm it. He made the smaller moon to brighten up the dark night sky. And all the twinkling stars appeared. On the fifth day God thought about the empty seas and lakes. They needed to be filled with fish. So He created giant whales and sleek sharks. He created shiny rainbow trout and goldfish and tiny guppies.

Then He filled the sky with birds. Screeching seagulls, busy hummingbirds, big-beaked toucans. At the end of the fifth day God looked at all He had created. It was good.

On the sixth day God created every kind of animal. Fat cows, shaggy yaks, woolly sheep, and yawning kitties. And then He made the most special part of His whole creation. God made a man. And He made a woman. God created the man and the woman to be His very special friends.

—LINDA PORTER CARLYLE

# THE PERFECT PRESENT

Adam and Eve's Creation Day celebration was the greatest party ever held. First Adam, newly alive, opened his eyes and looked into the face of God. Then God took him on a tour of his beautiful garden home. Friendly animals paraded before Adam. Thousands of daisies, violets, and orchids danced in the sunlight. Redwoods stretched to the sky, and robins warbled from their branches. A silvery river flowed through the center of the garden. Finally God gave Eve to Adam.

Now it was Eve's turn for surprises. She looked at God Himself and knew that He had made her. Then Eve looked deeply into Adam's delighted eyes and smiled.

"You are what I've been looking for," he told her. "You are a part of me, because you were made from my very bone."

Next God gave them a special gift—marriage.

Also, God said, "You are king and queen of all creation. Take care of the plants and animals in the garden, for it is yours to enjoy."

Adam and Eve explored the garden. Holding hands, they ran through a waterfall. Suddenly they stopped, startled by their reflections in a pond, then laughed at the surprised looks on each other's faces. They tried to count the different kinds of fruit dangling from scores of fruit trees, but decided it was much more fun simply to taste them! Tenderly

they touched the velvety petals of roses and lilies and carefully buried their noses in sweet-smelling honeysuckle. They stretched themselves on the carpet of deep, soft grass, their heads pillowed on the warm roundness of a purring tiger. Through the branches of a maple they gazed at the bright-blue sky.

As they talked the day away, something began to happen. The sky began to change from brilliant blue to pink, then lavender, next gold, and finally red. Adam and Eve hardly breathed. Constantly changing, the sky glowed and gleamed with golden fire; it blazed with red glory; it beamed with pink and purple splendor. And the sun, the great golden sun, began to slip from the sky. Down, down it slid, and as it lowered, it became red, redder—so red it bathed the whole garden with a rosy glow.

Then they heard a wonderful voice that made them feel free, happy, and loved. The Creator, more glorious than the glowing sky, stood before them. "What you see," He said, "is a sunset. It marks the end of the sixth day and the beginning of the seventh day of Creation. I am giving you the seventh day as a special present. On this day I will meet with you, and together we will remember Creation week. From sunset on the sixth day until sunset on the seventh day will be the Sabbath, a day of rest and celebration."

As the sun dipped below the meadow and as the stars came out, Adam and Eve and the Creator talked together. The couple had so many questions.

Were they the only beings whom God had created besides the animals? God told them about angels.

Why had God created this beautiful world when He already had a whole universe? Because they, Adam and Eve, were in His mind . . . and He loved them.

"Tell us," they begged, "what You made first."

God ended His work of Creation by setting aside the seventh day and blessing it and making it holy. That day of rest came to be known as "Sabbath," a Hebrew word that means rest.

So God told them what He had done on each day, explaining why He had created things in the order in which He did. Air and sunlight had to be there for the plants. Water had to be there for the fish to swim in and for the animals to drink. The land had to exist so the grass could grow and the animals could eat.

The next morning the golden sun climbed back into the sky, and every blade of grass, every shrub, leaf, and vine, sparkled with dew. And

**GENESIS 2:1-3**

So the sky, the earth and all that filled them were finished. By the seventh day God finished the work he had been doing. So . . . he rested from all his work. God blessed the seventh day and made it a holy day. He made it holy because on that day he rested. He rested from all the work he had done in creating the world.

**EXODUS 20:8-11**

"Remember to keep the Sabbath as a holy day. You may work and get everything done during six days each week. But the seventh day is a day of rest to honor the Lord your God. On that day no one may do any work: not you, your son or daughter, or your men or women slaves. Neither your animals nor the foreigners living in your cities may work. The reason is that in six days the Lord made

waiting for them in the garden was God.

Sabbath morning! Other than God's wonderful love itself, Adam and Eve knew that the Sabbath was the finest and best of all His gifts. Suddenly they heard music. It was not the songs of the birds, or the ripple of the river, or the loud rumble of a lion. Sweet and glorious, it rose and fell, then swelled again in a harmony so beautiful that the listeners felt their hearts would burst. Thousands of voices blended in an anthem of praise to their wonderful Creator.

everything. He made the sky, earth, sea and everything in them. And on the seventh day, he rested. So the Lord blessed the Sabbath day and made it holy

**PSALM 104:2-30**
You stretch out the skies like a tent. . . .

You built the earth on its foundations. . . .
You covered the earth with oceans. . . .
The mountains rose. The valleys sank. . . .
The earth is full of the things you made. . . .
You made the moon to mark the seasons.
And the sun always knows when to set. . . .

Lord, you have made many things.
With your wisdom you made them all. . . .
All these things depend on you. . . .
When you breathe on them, they are created.

Then Adam and Eve saw them—bright, shining beings, radiant with love and goodness, joyfully singing. Angels! Hardly knowing what they were doing, Adam and Eve opened their mouths and sang too. And God sang with them.*

All day long Adam and Eve explored their brand-new home with God. He led them to a mossy bank where a stream tumbled and gurgled over gold and silver stones. Coho salmon swam to the bank at the sound of their Creator's voice.

"How do they breathe?" asked Adam.

God explained the secrets of the water and the secrets of the air. Adam and Eve learned about oxygen. They learned about themselves and their lungs and their blood systems.

Eve wanted to know about the stars. "Let's start with the star nearest to you," God said. "That star is the sun." And He told her how the sun's rays traveled, how it was close enough to keep the earth just the right temperature—not too hot and not too cold.

Adam and Eve listened to all God said. But they wanted to learn more and more. God smiled at their eagerness. "Every Sabbath we shall meet together like this," He said softly. "And you have forever to learn new things!"

Then God led them to a hill all green and silver with softly swaying grasses. Sparkling steps led gently upward. Eagerly they climbed them. At the top of the hill they looked down on their garden home. Alive with color and movement and beauty, it shone like a giant jewel.

The first man and woman turned to their Creator. "Thank You for this beautiful present. We love You for all You have done!"

As the sun slid below the horizon and the stars twinkled in the skies, Adam and Eve lay down to watch the sky before going to sleep. The Sabbath! What a gift! They could hardly wait for the next one.

---

*Brand adds scenes and narrative not in Scripture to enhance the story line.

Can you imagine what it must have been like for Adam and Eve to explore their newly created world? Everything must have been full of surprises.

# The Perfect Present

Adam didn't even notice the huge lion that rubbed its head against his leg. He couldn't take his eyes off the beautiful wife God had given him.

God laughed. "This is your home," He exclaimed, His arms open wide. "It all belongs to you. And you belong to each other!"

Adam and Eve explored their wonderful garden home. They tasted plump, sweet blueberries for the very first time. And crisp, juicy red apples. They took long, sweet drinks from a tumbling stream. They raced with the deer across grassy meadows, and they giggled at waddling ducks.

Gradually the sky began to fill with glorious pink, and orange, and gold colors. The sun looked like it was sinking lower and lower. It disappeared behind the hills. "That is the sunset," God told them softly. "It tells us when the day ends. Go to sleep now. I will see you in the morning."

Just as He promised, God returned to the garden early in the morning. "This is Sabbath," God said. "We can spend the whole day together. I will tell you all about this new world I made."

Adam and Eve sat side by side on the thick green grass. They held hands and listened to all God had to say. They asked lots and lots of questions, and God answered every one.

Then company came. Bright angels sang beautiful songs of praise to God, and they taught Adam and Eve the words so they could sing along too.

Adam and Eve, God, and the angels picnicked together. They laughed together at the spider monkeys swinging from branch to branch. They lay on their bellies on the ground and watched the tiny ants.

"Is tomorrow Sabbath too?" Eve asked happily.

"No," God answered. "I am giving you one Sabbath every week. And they will all be wonderful!"

—Linda Porter Carlyle

# OUTLAWS AND OUTCASTS

Days flowed into perfect days in the beautiful Garden of Eden. But God had said one word that puzzled Adam and Eve. It had dropped like a strange, dark object into the sunlit garden—*die*. When God told them about the tree of the knowledge of good and evil, He had said, "If you ever eat fruit from that tree, you will die!"

Adam and Eve tried their best to imagine what it meant to die, but no living, breathing thing had ever died—not a wolf, not a robin, not a monarch butterfly.

Adam and Eve had heard one other strange thing. They'd heard about Lucifer. This once-honored angel, beautiful and intelligent beyond all others, had rebelled against God. Slowly but surely the outlaw angel had convinced other angels that God was unfair. God was patient and loving with Lucifer and his rebels, but they hardened their hearts and became more evil. God had to banish them from heaven. And he was then named Satan.

One day Eve followed a trail of bright-red flowers, picking them as she went. She would spread them as a carpet for Adam. Standing up straight, she noticed that she was in the center of the garden! And there was that tree of the knowledge of good and evil that God had told them about. *I wonder why God told us not to eat it,* Eve thought to herself.

"Did God really say that you must not eat fruit from any tree in the garden?" inquired an unfamiliar voice. Eve jumped. The voice seemed to be coming from the tree! A little frightened now, she looked closer; then she relaxed. It was only a serpent, one of those beautiful, golden-winged creatures that Adam had named.

Without thinking much about how a serpent came to be talking, Eve answered. "We may eat fruit from the trees in the garden. But God told us, 'You must not eat from the tree that is in the middle of the garden. You must not even touch it, or you will die.'"

"Eve, don't you know why God told you that? He doesn't want you to enter a higher order. He wants you to be forever imprisoned on a level where you cannot know what He knows. You are doomed, Eve, unless you eat some of this fruit. Why, just look what it has done for me!" The serpent paused to take another juicy bite. "Obviously, I'm not dead."

## BIG MISTAKE!

Gone from Eve's mind were the memories of God's wonderful gifts, of evening walks with Him, of shared sunsets and Sabbaths. Forgotten were the heavenly warnings against Satan, for it was Satan who was speaking to Eve, using the beautiful serpent as a disguise.

The pleasing voice continued. "You will not die. God knows that if you eat the fruit from that tree, you will learn about good and evil. Then you will be like God!" The serpent paused and then said, "Here, try some."

Eve's hand reached out . . . took the forbidden fruit. She raised it to her God-formed lips. The perfect teeth, so white and pure, pierced the flesh, and the juice spurted.

---

Scripture doesn't identify the forbidden fruit. Christian poet Commodianus (c. A.D. 250) thought it was an apple, because in Latin the word *malus* means both "evil" and "apple."

---

The golden serpent flew away. Eve stood, the fruit in her hand. She felt strangely excited. She was becoming wiser! Oh, Adam had to try this fruit!

She gathered all the fruit she could in her arms. Her eyes sparkled, and her cheeks burned as she called, "Adam! Adam! Look! . . . You know that tree we've been avoiding? Adam, I ate some, and it's . . . !"

Adam's face went pale. "You *what?*"

"Oh, Adam, don't look at me like that! I ate some, and I'm just

---

**GENESIS 3**

Now the snake was the most clever of all the wild animals the Lord God had made. One day the snake spoke to the woman. He said, "Did God really say that you must not eat fruit from any tree in the garden?"

The woman answered the snake, "We may eat fruit from the trees in the garden. But God told us, 'You must not eat fruit from the tree that is in the middle of the garden. You must not even touch it, or you will die.'"

But the snake said to the woman,

"You will not die. God knows that if you eat the fruit from that tree, you will learn about good and evil. Then you will be like God!" . . .

So she took some of its fruit and ate it. She also gave some of the fruit to her husband, and he ate it. . . .

Then they heard the Lord God walking in the garden. This was during the cool part of the day. And the man and his wife hid from the Lord God among the trees in the garden. But the Lord God called to the man. The Lord said, "Where are you?"

The man answered, "I heard you walking in the garden. I was afraid. . . . So I hid."

God said to the man, ". . . Did you eat fruit from that tree? I commanded you not to eat from that tree." . . . So the Lord God forced the man out of the garden of Eden. He had to work the ground he was taken from. God forced the man out of the garden. Then God put angels on the east side of the garden. He also put a sword of fire there. It flashed around in every direction. This kept people from getting to the tree of life.

Genesis 3:24 says that God placed cherubim with flashing, rotating swords east of Eden. In the ancient Near East, cherubim were depicted

fine! I didn't die; I've never felt better! Adam, you must try some!"

Adam stared at his wife, not quite able to grasp that Eve had eaten the fruit. God had told them not to. If they ate the fruit, they would die. But Eve wasn't dead! Eve stood before him, laughing, radiant, alive.

For just a moment God's loving face flashed in Adam's memory. He remembered the countless gifts that God had showered upon him and Eve. He recalled the warning, "Don't eat from the fruit of that tree . . ."

But Eve stood before him, smiling with her secret knowledge, sweet drops of nectar still glistening on

...s winged, composite creatures that were always associated with deity. Often they seem to function as guards.

her lips. Never had she looked more appealing. He must know Eve's secret. What knowledge brought that sparkle to her eyes? He seized the fruit, crushed it in his mouth, and swallowed.

Suddenly the sky grew dark, and the air grew chill. Adam's and Eve's naked bodies shivered with a cold they'd never before felt. Frightened and ashamed, the king and queen of Paradise skulked behind the bushes, trying to hide themselves.

And in heaven the angels cried, and the tears of God streamed in the universe. But Satan chortled.

Trying to hide themselves from each other and from God, Adam and Eve pulled large, flat fig leaves from a tree, sewed them together, and wrapped them around themselves. They knew that soon God would, as usual, stroll through the garden, ready for His evening visit with them. But for the first time they were not eager to see Him.

Then they heard Him calling them. Never before had He had to call them. Why were Adam and Eve not running to meet Him? Why were they frightened and ashamed? They had tasted sin. The poison of sin had separated them from God.

"Adam, what have you done?" God asked.

Adam, infected with the poison of sin, blamed God and his beloved Eve for what *he* had done! "*You* gave this woman to me. *She* gave me fruit from the tree. So I ate it."

"And you, Eve; what have you done?" God asked.

Eve, too, is ready to blame someone else for her sin. "Uh—the serpent tricked me," she stammered.

God knew already what Adam and Eve had done, of course. He had seen their every action and read their every thought. But how He had hoped that they would at least admit their sin!

Then God told them what would happen because of sin. Nothing would ever be quite the same.

He began with the serpent. "A curse will be put on you. . . . You will crawl on your stomach, and you will eat dust all the days of your life. I will make you and the woman enemies. . . . Her child will crush your head. And you will bite his heel."*

"And Eve, . . . although I created you as Adam's equal, because man now has sin in his nature, he will use his greater strength to rule over you. You will have children, but you will have great pain as you give birth."

"You, Adam, because you did not love Me enough to obey Me, will find that the earth will no longer bloom and grow like this garden. There will be thorns, weeds, and thistles. Growing food to eat will be difficult. You will sweat and grow weary until finally you will die and turn back into the dust from which you were made."

"And now," God continued, with tears still in His voice, "because you have known evil, because sin is now in you, you can no longer live here in Paradise and eat from the tree of life. You must leave. Now!"

Adam and Eve gazed for the last time on their Paradise home. Each valley and hill, each riverbank and lakeshore, each tree, each flower, each beloved animal, brought memories of love and laughter and shining innocence. But now it was not the same.

## GOD OFFERS HOPE

But God still loved them. He knew that they needed two things. They needed clothes, and they needed to know that their sins could be forgiven. Lovingly He fashioned for them clothing from the skins of precious animals. With shocked eyes and drained faces, Adam and Eve watched the blood spurt from the dying animals. And Eve remembered juice spurting from forbidden fruit while the words "you shall surely die" echoed in her mind.

God threw the tear-blinded couple out of Eden. He stationed at the gate a shining angel. Brilliant, blinding light beamed across the earth and sky as the angel held aloft a flaming sword.

It had been a day of sorrow, loss, and horror. It had been a day that would change each day that followed it.

But God did not leave them without hope. His love is bigger than sin and bigger than death. He Himself would crush the head of the serpent Satan. And as the animals' blood flowed so that the bodies of Adam and Eve could be covered, so His own blood would someday flow to cover their sins.

---

*Genesis 3:14, 15, ICB.

# Outlaws and Outcasts

Eve stared at the tall tree in the middle of the garden. Its fruit looked plump and juicy, but God had said not to eat the fruit from that tree.

"Have some fruit!" a soft voice said.

Eve looked around. Who was that talking? Could it be that beautiful snake in the tree?

"God said not to eat this fruit or we will die," Eve whispered.

"You won't die!" The serpent laughed. "You will become like God!"

Eve decided to believe the serpent. She tasted the fruit. Then she shared some with Adam. Adam also decided to eat the fruit—even though God had said not to.

Suddenly Adam and Eve felt ashamed. They wanted to cover themselves and hide. They pulled big fig leaves from the trees and sewed the leaves together to make clothes for themselves. Then they stayed among the thick bushes to hide from God, who came to see them.

"Where are you?" God called, walking in the garden.

"I was hiding," Adam answered.

"Did you eat the fruit I told you not to eat?" God asked.

"Yes, because Eve gave it to me!" Adam said.

"Did you eat the fruit I told you not to eat?" God asked Eve.

"Yes, because the snake gave it to me!" Eve answered.

God cried.

"You cannot live in the garden anymore," God said. "Your life will be hard now. And one day you will die."

Adam and Eve did not know what that meant. Nothing in the world had ever died.

"This is what death is," God said. He killed some animals. He used their skins to make clothes for Adam and Eve. Because of Adam's and Eve's sin, the animals died. And because of Adam's and Eve's sin, one day God's own Son would die for their sins. And for everyone's sins. Even yours.

—LINDA PORTER CARLYLE

# FIRST BIRTH—FIRST DEATH

Little drops of sweat stood out on Eve's forehead. Her eyes were wide with pain, and she bit her lip to hold back a scream. For months she had dreamed of having a baby. She had tried to imagine what it would look like, how it would feel to hold it, whether it would be a boy or a girl. Now all she could think of were God's words "When you give birth to children, you will have great pain."

Another pain tore through her belly, and suddenly Adam was holding a tiny form in his hands. A thin, reedy cry stabbed the air, and the third human being to occupy Planet Earth lived and breathed.

A smile spread across Eve's face. Forgotten was the pain. A baby, a baby boy, was hers to love and hold. Holding hands, Adam and Eve thanked God for their precious baby. He was so sweet, so little, so full of promise! Why, he might even be the one to crush the serpent's head, as God had pledged. Eve said, "I think we should call him 'Cain.'"

Adam and Eve had wondered about so many things. Would their newborn baby be able to walk around on wobbly legs, like a newborn calf? Would his eyes be closed like a newborn kitten's? How long would his hair be, or would he have hair? Would he have teeth? What would he sound like? Would he be able to talk?

Quickly they discovered that he was more helpless than any of the newborn animals

Cain means "one gotten" or "metalworker." Abel means "breath" or "fleeting—short-lived." Some scholars see in the tension between these two brothers a reflection of the strife marking gardeners and shepherds in ancient Middle Eastern society.

they knew. He must be carried and cuddled and fed and loved.

Cain grew quickly. Soon he could run around, and then he could talk. Adam and Eve loved to have him with them as they worked. His chubby hands could hold a bowl or pat a lamb. And always Adam and Eve told him stories about Eden. They told about the first Sabbath and of talking face to face with God. They told him that God loved them all and that God's Son would pay the price for their sins.

Soon Cain had a little brother. Adam and Eve named him Abel. Cain and Abel were the first children.

As Cain and Abel grew, they behaved differently. Cain often became grumpy and disobedient. He sometimes got tired of listening to the stories of Eden and of God. But Abel's eyes would shine and his mouth would smile as he pictured the sparkling river and the tree of life in the Garden of Eden. "Oh," he would exclaim, "I wish I could hear the angels sing, and talk to God face to face!"

And Adam and Eve would say, "Someday, dear child, God will make that possible!"

**GENESIS 4:1-16**

[Eve] became pregnant and gave birth to Cain. . . . After that, Eve gave birth to Cain's brother Abel. Abel took care of sheep. Cain became a farmer.

Later, Cain brought a gift to God. He brought some food from the ground. Abel brought the best parts of his best sheep. The Lord accepted Abel and his gift. But God did not accept Cain and his gift. Cain became very angry. . . .

The Lord asked Cain, "Why are you angry? . . . Sin wants you. But you must rule over it."

Cain said to his brother Abel, "Let's go out into the field." So Cain and Abel went into the field. Then Cain attacked his brother Abel and killed him.

Later, the Lord said to Cain, "Where is your brother Abel?" Cain answered, "I don't know. Is it my job to take care of my brother?"

Cain sometimes would go out into his garden or his vineyard, where he would sulk. At times he even wished Abel weren't around. "He thinks he's so great," he would mutter. Then he would start working. Cain had a knack for growing things. He would loosen the soil around the plants, he would pull weeds, and he would pull out some plants to give others more room to grow. Today we would say that he had a "green thumb." His bean plants grew tall, and his cucumbers grew big, and his grapevines sagged under the weight of giant clusters of juicy grapes.

Abel liked to take care of the animals. No one ever had to remind him to feed the calves or take water to the sheep. He loved them. When a sheep was ready to have a lamb, Abel would stay with her for hours to help her and to make sure that her baby was all right.

One thing that Cain and Abel always did together was to give an offering to God. Adam and Eve had taught them just how to do it. They explained that God wanted them to bring an offering to Him to show that they believed in His promise. That offering had to be an animal. It could not be clothes, or gold, or silver, or food, or pretty stones. It had to be something that would bleed and die, for the offering stood for the Son of God's own blood, the price for sin.

Each time Abel offered his sacrifice, his heart would nearly break as he watched an animal, perhaps one of his favorite little lambs, die. And he understood that sin, not just his parents' sin but his own,

caused such suffering. And he believed that just as an innocent animal must die, someday God's Son would also suffer and bleed and die.

Each time Cain brought an offering, his mind seethed with rebellious thoughts. Such a bother! Why did he have to bring an animal, anyhow? It would be easier for him to bring some of his own fruit. And as for sin—it wasn't his fault that his parents had eaten the forbidden fruit! Why couldn't he just do things his own way?

## THE FIRST MURDER

It was time once more for Cain and Abel to bring their offerings. Again Abel's heart was full. He wanted to show God that he loved Him. But as he looked at his flock he nearly cried to think that once more another lamb must die. Sin was such a terrible thing!

Abel chose the very best lamb as an offering. It was the firstborn of the flock, strong, healthy, perfect. Abel lifted it gently in his arms, his fingers sinking deep into its thick, oily wool. Then, with hands that trembled, he slaughtered it.

Cain walked slowly toward the flocks of animals. He stood a moment, looking at them with a hard eye. Then he turned and walked purposefully back toward his gardens. For once he would do things *his* way. Fruit was just as good as an animal. Quickly he picked and gathered some fine fruit, then dumped it next to Abel's offering.

The Bible tells us that "the Lord accepted Abel and his gift. But God did not accept Cain and his gift." There are places in the Bible that tell us God

Then the Lord said, "What have you done? Your brother's blood is on the ground. That blood is like a voice that tells me what happened. And now you will be cursed in your work with the ground. It is the same ground where your brother's blood fell. Your hands killed him. You will work the ground. But it will not grow good crops for you anymore. You will wander around on the earth."

Then Cain said to the Lord, "This punishment is more than I can stand! . . . You have forced me to stop working the ground. And now I must hide from you. I will wander around on the earth. And anyone who meets me can kill me."

Then the Lord said to Cain, "No! If anyone kills you, I will punish that person seven times more." Then the Lord put a mark on Cain. It was a warning to anyone who met him not to kill him. Then Cain went away from the Lord. Cain lived in the land of Nod.

Cain's grandson Irad may have founded Eridu, one of the first cities. Archaeologists uncovered a tablet they call "Eridu Genesis," which relates a Creation story.

has sent fire from heaven to show that He accepted an offering. Perhaps that is what He did for Abel, but not for Cain. In any case, Cain knew that God did not accept his offering.

All Cain's jealousy of Abel and all his resentment toward God came boiling to the surface. His face flushed, and his hands turned into hard fists. But he kept his voice low as he said to his brother, "Let's go out into the field."

So Abel and Cain walked out into a field. Then Cain no longer controlled himself. Screaming at Abel all his anger and jealousy and hatred, he suddenly turned on him and killed him.

Hastily Cain buried the body of his brother in the dirt, trying to cover his sin. Then God spoke to Cain, asking, "Where is your brother Abel?"

"I don't know. Is it my job to take care of my brother?"

Now God came right to the painful point. "Your brother's blood," He said, "is on the ground. That blood is like a voice that tells me what happened."

Cain looked startled as God continued: "Now you will be cursed in your work with the ground. . . . It will not grow good crops for you anymore. You will wander around on the earth."

"Oh!" whined Cain, suddenly afraid, but not sorry for his sin, "that's not fair! Everybody will be against me and try to kill me!"

"No!" said God tenderly. "If anyone kills you, I will punish that person seven times more."*

So God placed a special mark on Cain so that people would know that they must not raise a hand against him.

What sorrow there was in the home of Adam and Eve that night. Their precious son, Abel, dead! Their beloved Cain, whom they had hoped would be the promised one, the world's first murderer! They looked with pain on the face that since babyhood had so filled them with joy. With mixed feelings and many tears they watched him pack his things and walk away into the shadows.

Satan gloated! These humans had chosen him as their commander! Look how they kept sinning! But there were still those who loved God and obeyed Him and believed His promise. Satan would yet be overcome!

_____

*See Genesis 4:3-15, ICB.

# First Birth—First Death

Eve was filled with joy! She kissed the tip of her baby's little nose. She counted his tiny fingers and toes. He was absolutely perfect!

Adam watched her proudly. He knew just how she felt because he loved to cuddle their new baby too. Little Cain. Their very first son.

Cain grew quickly. He loved playing in the dirt and walking among the plants Adam took care of. "I think he will be a good farmer," Papa Adam said.

One day a second son was born to Adam and Eve. He was absolutely perfect too. Adam and Eve named him Abel.

Little Abel grew quickly. He loved running after the cute lambs in the fields. "I think he will be a good shepherd," Mama Eve said.

Adam and Eve told their boys stories about the beautiful garden where they had lived. They told their boys that they had eaten the fruit God said not to eat and that their sin had changed everything. They showed their boys how to worship God by sacrificing an animal. "The animal's blood reminds us that God's Son will die someday to save us," they said.

One day when Abel brought one of his best lambs as an offering to God, Cain decided to bring some of the food he had grown. God was happy with Abel's offering, but He was not happy with Cain's. This made Cain very, very angry. "Let's go for a walk," he said to Abel. And when they were out in a field, Cain killed his brother.

"What have you done?" God asked. "Now you must leave your home."

Adam and Eve felt so sad! They watched their son walk away from them. Sin was such a terrible thing! How much longer would they have to wait for God's Son to come and save them?

—LINDA PORTER CARLYLE

# THE MAN WHO WALKED INTO HEAVEN

Little Enoch climbed into Grandfather Adam's lap. Actually, Adam was more than Enoch's grandfather. He was more than his great-grandfather or even his great-great-grandfather. Adam was Enoch's grandfather counting back seven generations! In other words, Adam was Enoch's great-great-great-great-grandfather! You probably know your grandpa. But do you know your great-grandpa? Most children don't.

Enoch curled up into a comfortable ball and settled down for a story. He wondered which story Grandfather Adam would tell today, because Adam had lots of stories to tell of Eden and angels and of walking in the Garden of Eden with God. "Oh!" little Enoch would exclaim, "I wish I could walk with God like that!"

Then Grandmother Eve would hug him and say, "But you can! Just talk with God all the time! He hears you, and He is always with you, no matter where you go!"

As Enoch grew older, he remembered that. In fact, he thought about it all the time. And he started to take walks. With long strides he would climb to the top of a hill, trying to get as close to God as possible. While Enoch walked, he talked to God about everything, and God became his very closest and dearest friend.

One day when Enoch was walking and talking with God, he found himself near the Garden of Eden. The angel with the flaming sword still guarded the gate. Enoch

could not take his eyes away from the light. Its blazing golden beams seemed to draw him, yet he could not get close to it. Day after day Enoch returned to stare at that light.

When Enoch was about 60 years old, he got married. He and his wife worshipped God and welcomed Him into their new home.

Enoch thought his life couldn't possibly be any happier, but one wonderful day he became a daddy. A little boy with a long name brought Enoch and his wife a new understanding of God's love. Young Methuselah soon joined his daddy on his long walks. Enoch would boost him to his shoulders, and away they would go—into the woods, up the hills, across the streams, and to the entrance of the Garden of Eden.

Then Enoch would settle Methuselah on a bed of soft leaves while he turned his face to the light and talked with God. Methuselah could hear some of Enoch's words. He heard "Thank You," and he heard "I love you," and he heard questions and then long pauses, as if Enoch were listening to the answers to his questions. It seemed to Methuselah that Enoch never really started or ended a conversation with God; they just continued one long talk.

Little by little, people began to notice changes in Enoch. When he would return from his long walks, his face glowed with the same light that flashed from the angel's fiery sword. He was always ready to help others with their work or problems. More and more he told them things God had revealed to him about the future of the world and how much God loved them. He pleaded with them to turn from their sins so that they could someday live with their Creator.

## SURPRISE FOR ENOCH

As the years passed, Enoch spent even more time with God. Methuselah became a man, and Adam, noble Adam, died and was buried in the ground from which he had been formed.

People were sobered by Adam's death. He was, after all, their first father. He, unlike them, had looked into the face of God and had been shaped and molded by His very hand. Now Adam was dead.

Enoch wondered about death. He believed that God would someday bring His children home to live with Him. But he had never seen anyone go to live with God. Instead, they died and were buried in the ground, just as Adam had been. Enoch began to plead with God to help him understand.

Methuselah wasn't just sure when it happened, but he became aware that his father was moving closer to the light when he prayed to God. As Methuselah watched his father pray, it seemed that he was no longer part of this earth but part of heaven.

One day Methuselah walked with Enoch to that wonderful spot where the angel guarded the entrance to Paradise. As they walked along, Enoch spoke softly to his son. "Methuselah," he said with all the love in his voice he had always held for this dear son, "you're a full-grown man now of 300 years. I wish I could tell you how much I love you and how proud I am of you.

"When you were born, your mother and I thought we knew a lot about love, but you have

---

**GENESIS 5:18-24**

When Jared was 162 years old, he had a son named Enoch. After Enoch was born, Jared lived 800 years. During that time he had other sons and daughters. So Jared lived a total of 962 years. Then he died.

When Enoch was 65 years old, he had a son named Methuselah. After Methuselah was born, Enoch walked with God 300 years more. During that time he had other sons and daughters. So Enoch lived a total of 365 years. Enoch walked with God. One day Enoch could not be found, because God took him.

The angel portrayed in this illustration is a stereotypical Christian rendering. However, some traditions don't envision angels as having wings. Ancient Near Eastern cherubim were creatures made up of parts from different animal species.

taught us so much more. Because of you we have come to understand that no matter what we do, God will always love us, just as we will always love you no matter what you do. It's true that you can hurt us and sadden us by wrong actions, but you cannot destroy our love. It's like that with God, only much more so. He is eager to forgive us when we do wrong, happy to forget our sins when we repent.

"For all my life, but especially since you were born, Methuselah, I have walked with God. My heart and His have beat together, because we have agreed that I am His and He is mine.

"Continue that walk, son, when I am gone. . . . You will be happy that you did."

Methuselah felt a lump in his throat. Tears brimmed in his eyes as he hugged the dear man who had carried him on his shoulders years earlier.

"Dad," he choked, "I know you love me. I love

**JUDE 14, 15**

Enoch, the seventh descendant from Adam, said this about these people: "Look, the Lord is coming with thousands and thousands of his holy angels. The Lord will judge every person. He is coming to judge everyone and to punish all who are against God. He will punish them for all the evil they have done against him. And he will punish the sinners who are against God. He will punish them for all the evil things they have said against him"

The Bible tells us of only two people who never died—Enoch and Elijah.

you and I love God, but why do you talk of 'going'? You're in the prime of life! You should be around for another 600 years or so!"

Enoch smiled, but already his eyes were looking past Methuselah toward that holy light from the angel's sword. "I'll go on ahead," he whispered.

Touching Methuselah lightly on the shoulder, Enoch walked quickly toward the light. Methuselah heard Enoch's voice in eager, happy conversation with his Best Friend. Then the beams of light that flashed from the mighty sword seemed to explode in a dazzling splendor that made Methuselah hide his eyes. For miles around, the landscape was bathed in a blinding white pool of radiance. Slowly it faded. Methuselah rubbed his eyes. What had happened? The angel with the fiery sword still stood guard by the gate. Everything seemed the same, except . . . except that he did not hear Enoch's voice!*

Methuselah wasn't sure what to do. Perhaps Enoch was praying silently and should not be disturbed. Yet something had happened. Something was different. Hesitantly he stepped forward, but the beams from the angel's blade were too bright for him to bear. Quickly he looked at the spot where his father had worshipped. Bare. Empty. Gone.

Gone! His father was gone! He thought of calling his name, but knew it to be no use. His mind raced over their conversation, so recently concluded. His father had known! He had been telling him goodbye!

Methuselah raced home and told everyone he met that God had taken Enoch to live with Him! Some thought the story a trick and a lie. They searched everywhere for Enoch. Unbelievers even approached the entrance to the garden, but their careless words and mocking laughter died on their lips as they stood in the presence of that holy angel. Silently they slunk homeward.

Enoch's family and many others who loved God were joyful beyond words, for Enoch had shown them all that those who walk with God will someday walk with Him in heaven.

---

*The Bible does not tell us that Methuselah was with Enoch when God took Enoch to His home. He may have been there. For the sake of the story line, Brand has Methuselah alone with Enoch at that momentous time. Perhaps other people also saw Enoch snatched away. We just don't know.

# The Man Who Walked Into Heaven

When Enoch was born, Adam and Eve, his great-great-great-great-grandparents, were still alive. They told Enoch stories about the Garden of Eden.

"God will always love you," Adam said, "even when you make mistakes."

"Yes," Eve agreed, "God is a wonderful friend."

"I want to be God's friend too," Enoch said.

As Enoch got bigger, some of the other children asked him, "Why do you pray all the time?"

"I'll never stop talking to God," Enoch said. And he didn't.

Enoch grew up and got married. Later his wife had a baby boy named Methuselah. Enoch spent many hours teaching Methuselah about God.

Years passed, and Methuselah grew up, married, and had children of his own.

Then one day Adam died!

Enoch missed Adam, but he knew God would return one day to take all His friends to heaven. "God, I am looking forward to seeing Adam in heaven," Enoch prayed. "Until then I will trust You and wait patiently."

One day Enoch and Methuselah took a walk. "I love you, son," Enoch said.

"I love you, too," Methuselah said. He looked at Enoch, then stopped in surprise. Enoch's face glowed with a bright light Methuselah had never seen before!

Enoch smiled. "Son, God has asked me to come live with Him."

"Now? How can that be, Dad?"

"I don't know, but I know that whatever God does will be good."

Suddenly Enoch and Methuselah saw and heard an explosion of light and sound. Methuselah shut his eyes tight. When he opened them again, Enoch was . . . gone!

Methuselah raced home, telling everyone that Enoch had gone to live with God. Some people were sad. Others were excited. Now they knew that God's special friends would someday walk with God in heaven!

—HEATHER GROVET

# NOAH BUILDS A BOAT

God was sad. He was more than sad. He felt such pain and sorrow that the Bible says He was "grieved." There had been such joy when He created Planet Earth and the first man and first woman. There had been such pleasure in thinking of the children who would be born to them and who would grow up living in a perfect, unspoiled paradise.

But all that had changed, of course. There had been that first sin, and from then on people had grown more and more wicked. Yes, there were always some who loved God and obeyed Him. Remember Enoch and Methuselah? But with every day that passed, fewer and fewer people honored Him.

God's love for everyone—good and bad—made Him grieve. His hatred of sin forced Him to make a decision. Sin and sinners must be destroyed. But God did not want anyone to be destroyed. "I must warn them," He declared. So God called a man named Noah. Noah lived for God and walked with Him just as his great-grandfather Enoch had done. God knew that He could trust Noah to obey Him and to follow His directions, no matter what.

"Noah," He said, "build [an ark] of cypress wood for yourself. Make rooms in it and cover it inside and outside with tar."

Noah wasn't quite sure what a "flood" was. There had never been a flood. There had

never even been rain, for God watered the earth with heavy dew.

Noah wasn't quite sure what an "ark" was, either. He'd undoubtedly seen small boats on the lakes, but this ark that God was talking about would be bigger than any boat he'd ever seen!

Noah, however, didn't ask questions. He obeyed. Following God's directions, he drew up plans for the ark. It would look something like a house, he mused, three stories high, with different rooms for different things. There would be a special very large area with stalls for the animals. There would be something like a skylight in the roof of the ark, but no other windows, and only one door. God had told him to use cypress wood, which is almost as hard as stone, one that will not rot for centuries.

Noah began to work. Trees as large as great towers had to be cut down. Then the wood had to be sawed into boards of just the right sizes. Everything had to fit perfectly. This ark had to be the strongest ship yet to be built.

Before long the huge stacks of lumber around Noah's house began to attract attention.

"Hey, Noah!" people would call. "What are you building, a barn?"

Then Noah would turn from his work, look them straight in the eye, and say urgently, "No. I'm building a big boat, a place of safety. God is going to destroy the world with a flood, but those who wish to serve Him may enter the ark I am building, and they will be safe."

"AN ARK? A FLOOD? Noah, you've been out in the sun too long! You're as crazy as an ostrich!" They would go on their way, shaking their heads and laughing.

But Noah kept on working. And he kept on talking with God. And the more he talked with God, the less he cared that people were laughing at him. He longed only for people to love God and turn from their sins.

Soon after God told Noah to build an ark, Noah and his wife had children. First little Japheth was born, then Shem, then Ham. Soon the three boys were big enough to help their father. They worked and worked. And from their father and mother they learned about God and learned to love Him.

When Shem, Ham, and Japheth became young men, they began to look for wives. It was not easy to find young women who loved God, because the beautiful young women around them worshipped idols and laughed at the God of heaven. But Shem, Ham, and Japheth each found a lovely young woman who loved God.

Now Noah and his wife, their three sons and their wives, all worked together on the ark, and Noah con-

> NOAH AND HIS WIFE, THEIR THREE SONS AND THEIR WIVES, ALL WORKED TOGETHER ON THE ARK, AND NOAH CONTINUED TO PREACH.

**GENESIS 6:5-22**

The Lord saw that the human beings on the earth were very wicked. . . . The Lord was sorry he had made human beings on the earth. His heart was filled with pain. So the Lord said, "I will destroy all human beings that I made on the earth. And I will destroy every animal and everything that crawls on the earth. I will also destroy the birds of the air. This is because I am sorry that I have made them." But Noah pleased the Lord. . . .

[God said to Noah], ". . . Build a boat of cypress wood for yourself. . . . I will bring a flood of water on the earth. I will destroy all living things. . . . But I will make an agreement with you. You, your sons, your wife and your sons' wives will all go into the boat. Also, you must bring into the boat two of every living thing, male

tinued to preach. And the people continued to poke fun at him. But Noah kept on preaching. And the believers in God kept working on the ark and ignoring the insults of those about them.

Years went by. The boat now had taken shape. It was a monstrous thing, dwarfing all the buildings around it. It was 450 feet long—one and a half times as long as today's football field. It was shaped in such a way that anyone would know it was meant to float on water. But what water? There wasn't enough water anywhere around to float the enormous ship.

Noah's preaching became more and more urgent. Surely, any time now, God would send water from the sky to float the ark. Any time now, people must repent. But the more he

# OTHER ANCIENT NEAR EASTERN FLOOD STORIES

The Genesis flood story was not the only ancient account of a deluge.

In the Atrahasis epic the human race became so many and so noisy that the gods could not sleep. The gods attempted to correct the situation through plagues, drought, a buildup of salt in the soil, and famine. But the problem remained. Finally the god Enlil decided to send a deluge. Ea, another god, was fond of a man named Atrahasis and saved his life by instructing him how to construct a vessel that he could enter to ride out the storm. The storm raged seven days and nights. Afterward Atrahasis offered sacrifices to the gods.

In the Epic of Gilgamesh, Utnapishtim survived the flooding of the city Shuruppak. Enlil had persuaded the council of gods to destroy Shuruppak and everything in it. But Ea sent a dream to Utnapishtim, telling him to build a cube-shaped craft. Ea directed him to load into it "the seed of life of all kinds" as well as his family and skilled artisans. The storm was so

This copy of the Atrahasis epic was found at Sippar in southern Iraq. It dates from the seventeenth century B.C.

powerful that the gods "cowered like dogs." Seven days after Utnapishtim's craft landed on Mount Nisir he sent out a dove, a swallow, and a raven. After he left his vessel he sacrificed to the gods.

Another Flood story appears in a Sumerian Creation account. Ziusudra, a pious king, heard a voice telling him that the assembly of the gods had decided to send a flood "to destroy the seed of mankind" and that Ziusudra should build a boat. The flood lasted seven days. The sun god Utu then shed his rays on the craft, and Ziusudra opened a window to let the light in. The human king then slew an ox and sheep as an offering. The gods Anu and Enlil re-created the vegetation.

Although we notice parallels between these flood stories and the Genesis account, we also find differences. God did not destroy humanity because of the racket they made, but because of their immorality (Genesis 6:5-7). Genesis recognizes the existence of only one God, not a host of squabbling deities. Noah did not receive immortality, as Utnapistim and Ziusudra did, and eventually died.

and female. Keep them alive with you. . . . Also gather some of every kind of food. Store it on the boat as food for you and the animals." Noah did everything that God commanded him.

**GENESIS 7:5-10**

Noah did everything that the Lord commanded him.

Noah was 600 years old when the flood came. He and his wife and his sons and their wives went into the boat. They went in to escape the waters of the flood. The clean animals, the unclean animals, the birds and everything that crawls on the ground came to Noah. They went into the boat in groups of two, male and female. This was just as God had commanded Noah. Seven days later the flood started.

Terminology used only once in Scripture is called *hapax legomenon*. The King James Version translators didn't know what the Hebrew wor

preached, the less that people listened.

At times Noah would go to bed at night, his hands blistered and hurting, and his muscles aching from wrestling with the heavy lumber, his throat sore from talking to people who didn't want to hear him. At times a small, dark thought would drift into his mind and say, *Do you really know what you're doing, Noah? Do you really think you are right while the whole world is wrong?* But he would push aside these thoughts and ask God to talk to him. And God would say,

"I am with you, Noah. Trust Me." And Noah trusted.

One clear and sunny day something happened that people had never seen before. From the forest at the edge of town, animals emerged. They didn't dart into the clearing, then race away. They stepped out as if they were in a parade. Some came in pairs; some in sevens. All behaved as though someone was commanding them.

People stood back in amazement. The shaggy woolly mammoth was there, the shy ibex, the beautiful white

meant, so they merely transliterated it as "gopher" wood. The term is related to Sumerian *giparu*, a kind of wood, but we don't know what kind.

oryx. There were goats and squirrels, lions and coneys, gazelles and leopards. All kinds of animals were there.

Then while people were still gasping at the strange sight, a huge shadow fell over the land and a gentle wind was felt as hundreds of birds blotted the sun from the sky in their flight toward the ark. The cries of ravens, the honking of geese, the warble of thrushes, blended with the sound of whirring wings. Below them, ostriches ran on their lanky legs, trying to keep up with their airborne cousins.

Fear gripped the people. Had Noah been right?

Noah sensed that people might at this time be ready to listen. He pleaded with them. "Please, dear friends, turn your backs on sin and enter the ark while there is still time. You see that the animals are entering even as we speak. God wants to do the same for you, but He will not force you to enter! Won't you come in and be saved?" Tears filled Noah's eyes as he pleaded.

Suddenly someone in the crowd moved. A

Genesis 6:3 says people would live for 120 years. This may refer to how long it took to build the ark. Others think it predicted the maximum life span that would finally prevail following the Flood. The first option is the more likely one.

young woman started forward, but a friend with her whispered, "Zilpah![1] What are you doing? You can't go in there with all those animals! Look, the sun is shining as brightly as ever!" Zilpah laughed self-consciously and stepped back.

Another started forward, an old man. "I've lived a sinful life," he muttered. But his children grasped his sleeves and held him. "Father! Don't make a fool of yourself! You'll embarrass us!" The old man turned away.

And so it went. Many people *almost* entered the ark. But no one did—other than Noah, his wife, his three sons, and his three daughters-in-law.

One hundred twenty years had passed since God

first spoke with Noah. One hundred twenty years of perfect weather, of brilliant sunshine, of kindly dew. Never had there been even a dark cloud in the sky. However, on one such beautiful day God said, "It's time, Noah. Go with your family into the ark." So eight faithful people walked silently into the bulky boat. "Then the Lord closed the door behind them."[2]

---

[1] Although Zilpah is a good Hebrew name and is found in the biblical story about Jacob and Laban, in this story Zilpah and her friend are like movie "extras." The same is true of the nameless "old man" and his children. Brand has written them into the story line to create a sense of immediacy.
[2] Genesis 7:16, ICB.

# Noah Builds a Boat

I feel very sad," God told Noah. "My people are bad. Almost no one loves Me anymore."

"I love You," Noah told God.

"You are like your great-grandfather, Enoch," God said. "That's why I want you to build a big boat."

"I will obey You. But what is the boat for?"

"I am going to cover the entire world with water," God explained. "Everyone inside the ship will stay safe."

Noah followed God's directions. Noah made the boat of strong wood. It stood as tall as a three-story house. "Make a window in the roof," God said, "and only one door."

Noah's neighbors laughed at him. "You are crazy," they teased.

"God is going to send a great flood," Noah explained. "He wants to save everyone in this boat."

"A flood!" they laughed. "Never!"

Before long Noah and his wife had three sons, Japheth, Shem, and Ham. The boys grew up and married three good women. The whole family worked together on the huge ship.

It took many years to make the large boat. "I will keep trusting God," Noah said.

Then one day something amazing happened. Animals—big and small—began marching toward the big boat.

Horses. And mice and bears and monkeys. God's angels made the animals enter the boat. Lions and elephants.

Then great flocks of birds flew into the ship—crows and pigeons and parrots and ducks.

The people became afraid. "Maybe Noah was right!" someone shouted. "Maybe there will be a flood."

Noah begged the people to enter the boat, but they all turned away.

God told Noah and his family to enter the boat. They walked inside, and the Lord shut the big door behind them.

Now they waited to see what God would do next.

—HEATHER GROVET

# GOD WASHES THE WORLD

For seven days—one long week—Noah and his family stayed inside the ark while the sun shone brightly outside. Children laughed and threw rocks and sticks at the ark. People swarmed around the huge boat, shouting insults.

Then one clear morning as people mocked, a dark cloud galloped across the sky, chased by a roaring wind. A blinding zigzag of light, an earsplitting crash, a darkening sky, and the earth trembled. Huge drops of water splattered from the sky, then fell in sheets. Terrified, people turned toward the big boat, begging, "Noah, let us in! Let us in! Please let us in!" But he could not. The Lord had shut the door, and only the Lord could open it.

Can't you just see the people running to the altars where they had sacrificed to their gods? "Help us! Help us!" they cried. But the altars now stood in mud. Tipping crazily, they soon toppled over and fell apart.

Water—walls of water—poured from the sky. Streams overflowed their banks. Once-peaceful lakes churned and spilled across the land. As the water rose, it began to fill houses and beautiful temples. People cried as they scrambled to the roofs of their houses. They screamed with every flash of lightning and every clap of thunder. You know how scary it can be in a storm, but imagine how frightening it must have been way back then,

because no one had ever seen or heard a thunder-and-lightning storm before this one. Some of them cursed with anger and defeat as they watched the wooden head of a useless idol go floating by.

The thought must have crossed their minds: *Why didn't we listen to Noah? Why did we listen to our friends who told us this could never happen?*

The waters rose higher and higher. In addition to the rain and the wind, earthquakes sent tremors across the land, and large fissures opened in the ground. Underground streams erupted and spewed into the air like upside-down waterfalls. And huge boulders shot into the air, landing with deadly force.

The only safe place was inside the ark. Tossing on the angry waters like a wood chip in a hurricane, it climbed high on the wave crests, and then slammed into the troughs. The strong cypress timbers creaked and moaned. The small animals squealed with terror. The big animals roared and trumpeted. The birds squawked. Green with seasickness, Noah and his family huddled together and prayed.

## HOPE DURING THE STORM

For 40 days and 40 nights the storm raged. The earth seemed to be turning inside out. The waters rose above the peaks of the highest hills.

Some hillsides yielded to the terrific force of the waters and crumbled into the seething waves. Tons of ruins—boulders, muck, sludge, sand—tumbled about in the mighty floodwaters, burying people, animals, giant trees, and other reminders of a world completely infected with evil.

The Creator's sadness overflowed like the drowning planet. He had made great plans for Adam's descendants, but they had chosen wickedness and death. And just as this planet was awash in water when God had begun creating, now He was returning it to that original condition. But this would not be the end of Planet Earth. God had in mind a new beginning. Inside that ark, made by Noah and watched over by angels, rode eight people who loved Him. They would help rebuild a new and happier world.

At last the bulky ship came to rest on the mountains of Ararat. The upset stomachs that Noah and his family had endured for so long began to feel better. But still the door was not opened. Noah's little family was restless. They had suffered seasickness far worse than you may have felt when you got carsick. Their muscles ached from trying to stand upright on the heaving floors while carrying feed to the animals. The crashing of waves and moaning of wind had stabbed their fitful sleep. Now they could rest—

> INSIDE THE ARK, MADE BY NOAH AND WATCHED OVER BY ANGELS, RODE EIGHT PEOPLE WHO LOVED GOD. THEY WOULD HELP REBUILD A NEW AND HAPPIER WORLD.

**GENESIS 7:6-21**

Noah was 600 years old when the flood came. . . .

Noah and his wife, his sons Shem, Ham and Japheth, and their wives went into the boat. . . . Then the Lord closed the door behind them.

Water flooded the earth for forty days. . . . All living things . . . died.

**GENESIS 8:1-21**

God made a wind blow over the earth. And the water went down. . . . [The boat] came to rest on one of the mountains of Ararat. . . .

Forty days later Noah opened the window he had made in the boat. He sent out a raven. . . . Then Noah sent out a dove. . . . The dove could not find a place to land. . . . So it came back to the boat. . . . .

and sleep. They began to feel normal again.

Climbing to the window of the ark, Noah opened it. From a cage he lifted a raven and released it to the sky. It was happy to be out of the ark, and quickly flew away.

He also tossed a dove into the air. *Ah,* he thought, *this bird will tell me when there is dry land.* But the dove, finding no place to rest, returned to the boat.

Later he sent out the dove a second time. This time it brought back a wonderful sign of life—a green olive leaf! Something had begun growing again!

Still later he once more sent out the dove. When it did not return, he decided that it must have found a place to build a nest. But still the Lord did not open the door.

More than seven long months after the ark

came to rest, God finally said, "Come out of the ark." The door swung open, and eight eager and thankful people walked safely out onto dry ground.

After seven days Noah again sent out the dove. . . . It came back to him with a fresh olive leaf in its mouth. . . . . Seven days later he sent the dove out again. But this time it did not come back.

Noah was now 601 years old. . . .

God said to Noah, "You and your wife, your sons and their wives should go out of the boat. . . .

So Noah went out with his sons, his wife and his sons' wives. . . .

Then Noah built an altar. . . . [God] said, . . . "I will never again destroy every living thing on the earth as I did this time."

GENESIS 9:13-17

"I am putting my rainbow in the clouds. It is the sign of the agreement between me and the earth. . . .

"[The rainbow] is the sign of the agreement that I made with all living things on earth."

But how different the world looked from the way they remembered it! Where were the beautiful rolling hills? Where were the tall, tall trees that rose into the sky like towers? And where were the beautiful flowers as big as Adam's hand?

Eagerly the animals streamed from the ark, sniffing the air and then bounding away on stiff legs.

Noah gathered his family about him. "Let us thank God," he said, "for His wonderful care over us."

So they built an altar right there, just eight people in a barren world, and offered sacrifices to God.

Noah and his family had been in the ark for more than a year. Now they needed to get on with their lives. God told them to have children. He blessed the land and promised that crops would again grow and fruit would again hang heavy in the trees.

But no more would the land be as it was in the days before the Flood. Sometimes, God said, dark clouds would appear and rain would fall. Then the people were to remember the Flood that had destroyed the world, but they were not to be afraid.

Noah looked to the sky and saw a banner of beautiful colors stretched from one horizon to the other. Glowing shades of red, orange, yellow, green, blue, and violet curved across the sky and filled him with wonder.

"Come quickly!" he called, and everyone came running as he pointed silently to the sky.

Then God spoke. "That's called a rainbow," He said. "It is a sign of My promise to you that I will never again destroy the whole earth with a flood."

The rabbis said that only the zebach tôdâ (sacrifice of gratitude)—like the one Noah offered—would be offered in the world to come.

# God Washes the World

People laughed at Noah's family inside the ark. Nothing had happened for a whole week. No rain. No flood!

Then one day thick black clouds blew in front of the sun. Thunder crashed. Rain poured down.

People screamed, "Noah, let us into your boat!"

But it was too late. Noah could not open the door.

The floodwaters grew deeper and deeper. Earthquakes shook the ground. Water squirted upward. Finally water covered everything.

"Don't be afraid," Noah told his family as the boat creaked, tossing up and down. "God will protect us."

God felt very sad. "Why wouldn't the others come onto My ship? I wanted to save them, too."

It rained 40 days. Even after the rain had stopped, the big boat floated atop the lonely sea. After many months the ship came to rest in the Ararat moun-tains. Noah climbed to the top of the boat and opened the window.

"Fly out," Noah said, letting loose a raven. The bird did not return.

Next Noah let a dove go, but it could not find a safe place to land.

Noah let the dove fly away a week later. This time the bird brought back a green leaf in its beak. "Plants are growing!" Noah rejoiced.

Noah waited one more week, and let the dove go again. This time it built a nest in the trees.

Finally God spoke to Noah, "You can come out."

How excited the animals were as they raced away across the earth! Noah and his family were very happy too.

Noah built an altar. He thanked God for saving their lives.

"Look!" someone called. In the sky was a beautiful rainbow—red, orange, yellow, green, blue, and violet.

"The rainbow is My promise to you," God said. "I will never flood the whole earth again."

—HEATHER GROVET

# "WHAT DID YOU SAY?"

Waraza,* tall, sun-bronzed, and with a mane of silver hair, stood before the citizens of Shinar.

The crowd buzzed like bees in a giant beehive. "What do you think Waraza has to say?" they asked one another. "Why do you think he called this special meeting of the town council?"

At last Waraza raised one majestic hand, and silence filled the room.

"My friends," Waraza spoke in the warm, deep tones the people loved, "I have asked you to meet today because I have an idea I want to share with you!"

The people leaned forward expectantly. As leader of the town council, Waraza constantly surprised them with his ideas.

"You all know," he continued, "how great we have become! Our shops are busy, our barns bulge with grain, our artists and craftsmen produce the finest work in the world! We are powerful and rich. In fact, we are the greatest people that ever were, or ever will be. Am I right?"

The people roared their agreement, clapped their hands, and laughed. The more Waraza talked, the more they understood just how great they really were, and their chests puffed out with pride.

"But, friends," Waraza lowered his voice to a stage whisper, a note of sorrow delicately edging his words, "when we die as others before us have, who will remember our greatness? Who will speak your name or mine and remember the days when we ruled the earth? No one, my friends, no one!" Waraza's words lingered in the air, and his listeners clutched their hearts at the fearful vision.

Waraza knew that he had their attention and that they liked his every word. He smiled a secret inner smile at how easily he could get these people to do anything he wanted just by his skillful use of words. He continued: "The gods have been good to us. Let us build a tower to reach into the heavens! We must build a tower worthy of us! We shall construct a tower whose top will swim in the clouds, so that our children, and their children, and all generations to come may know that we who live this day are the greatest mortals ever to have walked the earth."

The crowd could hardly stand it, so moved were they by the idea of a tower reaching to the sky, telling everyone how great they were.

"Let's build that tower! Let's build that tower!" they cried.

Waraza smiled and again held up one majestic hand. "My friends," he purred, "I knew you would want to build a tower that will last forever so that our names will always be remembered!"

God looked down on the foolish, proud people. In spite of the Flood, now many years past, people had chosen to forget Him. They worshipped ugly statues, and little ornaments that they made with their own hands. They built tower after tower, believing that the "gods" would come down and stay in them.

And now they proposed to build on the plain of Shinar a mighty tower that would say, "We don't need God. We're greater than He is." God whispered to Himself, "Oh, when will people return My love and let Me make them happy?"

Waraza called the best architect to draw the plans for the tower.

"This is how we'll build it," explained the architect. "We will build it in seven stages. The first stage will be a huge square. Each of the following squares will be higher and smaller than the one below it. A wide ramp will lead to the top of the tower, and on each side of the ramp will be a set of stairs. Climbing right up the center of the tower will be another set of stairs!" (Today we know such ancient tower temples by the name *ziggurat*.)

The people's eyes grew round and shiny as they

**GENESIS 11:1-9**

At this time the whole world spoke one language. Everyone used the same words. As people moved from the East, they found a plain in the land of Babylonia. They settled there. . . .

They said to each other, "Let's make bricks and bake them to make them hard." So they used bricks instead of stones, and tar instead of mortar. Then they said to each other, "Let's build for ourselves a city and a tower. And let's make the top of the tower reach high into the sky. We will become famous. If we do this, we will not be scattered over all the earth."

The Lord came down to see the city

pictured the huge tower, reaching for the sky.

Everyone got busy. They formed bricks from the clay soil. They baked them in a fire to make them extra hard, and gathered bitumen, a sticky oil—a kind of tar—to use as mortar. Maybe it took a whole year just to make the bricks. I don't know.

If people grew a little tired, Waraza lifted their spirits with honeyed words. If some became discouraged, he stirred them with an inspiring speech and thrilled them with a vision of their own greatness.

Finally the day came to lay the first brick. Children crowded in front of their parents so

and the tower that the people had built. The Lord said, "Now, these people are united. They all speak the same language. This is only the beginning of what they will do. They will be able to do anything they want. Come, let us go down and

confuse their language. Then they will not be able to understand each other."

So the Lord scattered them from there over all the earth. And they stopped building the city. That is where the Lord confused the language of the whole world.

So the place is called Babel. So the Lord caused them to spread out from there over all the whole world.

# HOW DO I SAY . . . ?

Here's how you'd write "Happy Birthday" in
Albanian: Urime ditelindjen!
Basque: Zorionak!
Chinese (Mandarin): Qu ni sheng er kuai Je
Danish: Tillykke med fodselsdagen!
Hawaiian: Hau'oli la hanau!
Maori: Kia huritau ki a koe!
Yoruba (Nigeria): Eku Ojobi!

Here's "Hello" in
Afrikaans: Hallo
Croatian: Bok
Hindi: Namaste

Marshallese: Iakwe (Yokwe)
Serbian: Zdravo
Swahili: Jambo
Yiddish: sholem aleychem

Ah, but now it's time to say "Goodbye" in
Armenian: Menak Parov
Dutch: Tot ziens
Finnish: Näkemiin

Indonesian: Sampai jumpa
Russian: Do svidaniya
Tagalog: Paalam
Xhosa: Sala kakuhle

How many times has your mother told you to say "Please"—in
Ainu (Japan): Wa enkore
Breton: Mar plij
Cree: Mâhti
Dyula (Mali): Sabari
Esperanto: Bonvolu
French: S'il vous plaît
Zulu: Jabulisa

And when you get what you asked for, you're supposed to say "Thank you" in
Abenaki: Wliwni
Gaam: Àayyá
Hmong Daw: Ua tsaug
Kuna: Dot nuet
Luganda: Webale
Ojibwe: Miigwech
Swedish: Tack

Finally, what about "Merry Christmas and Happy New Year"?
German: Froehliche Weihnachten und ein glückliches Neues Jahr!
Ilocano: Naimbag a Pascua ken Naragsac nga Baro nga Tawen!
Sicilian: Bon Natali e Prosperu Annu Novu!
Yupik: Quyanalghii Kuusma & Quyangalleq Nutaghamun Aymiqulleq
Got it?

as a prince might pluck a flower. Then, with a flourish, he laid it on the corner of the foundation. The people clapped wildly.

Then the work began in earnest. Laborers scurried back and forth, carrying baskets of mortar and loads of bricks. Foremen shouted messages to runners. "Go over to the east side and tell them we need more bricks!" "Don't send any more mortar; we have enough!"

The tower began to take shape. Soon it could be seen for miles around. It climbed higher and higher, and from the ground the workers at the top looked like little moving statues.

As the tower grew higher the people grew prouder. But some, a very few, still loved

they wouldn't miss anything! Waraza strutted around, smiling kindly at the children, basking in the admiring looks from the citizens of Shinar. Then he stepped forward, his silver hair shining in the sunlight. Moving gracefully, he picked up a brick

God and worshipped Him. They were afraid of what a proud, powerful people might do to those who were weaker.

All this time God had been watching the plans and actions of these people who had turned their backs on

Him. He had seen their pride and their cruelty toward others. He had seen how they cheated one another to get what they wanted. He had watched as their government grew stronger and stronger until it had finally turned into one big city of rebellion.

And He saw the plain of Shinar with its tower sticking up toward heaven. It was like a foolish child sticking out its tongue at God!

God saw one other thing. Everyone in the world spoke the same language at that time, and God saw that understanding each other's words stuck these rebellious people together just as mortar stuck their bricks together.

The Bible says that God came down to see what they were doing. He no longer simply watched, but decided to act. The God who created all things now created new languages, and in a flash the proud builders of a heathen tower were helpless to continue.

Waraza was strolling around an upper level of the tower when he heard a foreman yell, "Irrush ummane eli sha um pani!"

Everyone within earshot stopped and stared at the foreman. The foreman's face turned red. "I said I need more workers over here!" he yelled in a language that no one could understand. The workers stared at him with their mouths open.

"What did you say?" some called, but they couldn't even understand each other's question.

Waraza cleared his throat. "Harummph! Harummph!" It seemed some of these laborers were having trouble communicating. Well, he would soon straighten out the trouble. As soon as he spoke to them in his silken tones and eloquent

## THE GOD WHO CREATED ALL THINGS NOW CREATED NEW LANGUAGES, AND IN A FLASH THE PROUD BUILDERS OF A HEATHEN TOWER WERE HELPLESS TO CONTINUE.

words, everyone would get back to work.

Holding up his famed and majestic hand, he began to speak. "Sulummu ina birinni lishakin!"

Why was everyone staring at him so strangely? Why were they not smiling as the light of understanding dawned? Why were they looking at him as if they hadn't the slightest idea what he was talking about?

He tried once more. "Nimdaggara lahamesh!"

No one listened to him! Workers on the tower began to scream and throw things. Baskets of mortar came tumbling down. Fights broke out. In anger, fear, and despair, people ran down the steps of the tower, searching, speaking in strange new languages.

The confused people *did* find those who understood them, for God lovingly gave families the same language. Those who spoke the same language banded together and moved far away from those whom they could not understand. A kind God gave people the opportunity once again to make a new start in new parts of the world. He hoped that at last they would turn to Him!

And left behind on the plain of Shinar was the deserted tower. The tower of pride had become a monument to the foolishness of people who rebel against God.

---

*Waraza was the name of a real man talked about in an Old Babylonian document. He is not mentioned in the Bible. Like a movie "extra," he and the unnamed architect have been added to the story and given words to speak. Someone had to come up with the idea to build the Tower of Babel, and someone had to design it. Brand has chosen to name the one individual Waraza, to make the story more realistic, and to leave the other without a name.

# "What Did You Say?"

Noah's flood had happened many years earlier. Noah's family had grown until people covered the land again. Some of them remembered God, but many were too proud to think of anyone but themselves.

"We are a strong and mighty people," they said. "We don't need God."

Handsome Waraza was their leader. One day he had an idea. "Attention," Waraza announced. "We should build a very tall tower that will reach up to heaven! It will prove that we are the greatest people ever!"

The crowd clapped and cheered.

But God was sad. "Why won't they love Me? I would make them happy."

Waraza drew a picture of the tower. "We will use strong bricks and glue them together with tar. We can do this without God's help!"

The people began working.

"I need more bricks," someone yelled. "Get some more tar," another called. The tower grew taller . . . and . . . taller.

God was very upset. The people could all speak the same language, but it was full of angry and hateful words. They were so busy being proud that they didn't think of Him.

God decided to stop the people. He created many new languages so that each family spoke in different words and couldn't understand their neighbors.

Handsome Waraza tried to tell the workers what to do. "Sulummu ina birinni lishakin!" he called. But no one understood him.

He tried once more. "Nimdaggara lahamesh!" he ordered. But no one understood him.

The workers began to scream and yell. Finally they threw down their tools and rushed back to their homes. People who spoke the same languages moved away together, leaving the unfinished tower behind.

"I hope the people will now love Me," God said, "because I love them so very much."

—HEATHER GROVET

# MOUNT ARARAT

According to Scripture, Noah's ark "came to rest on the mountains of Ararat" (Genesis 8:4, NRSV)—perhaps the highest area in ancient Mesopotamia. Recent attempts to find the remains of the ark have concentrated on Mount Ararat even though it is a single volcanic mountain isolated on a plain.

Right: During the eleventh and twelfth centuries of the present era the mountain in this photo, sometimes called Mount Ararat, was deemed to be the place where the ark was grounded.

Left: In 1840 volcanic Mount Ararat—16,945 feet above sea level—erupted. The rocks in this picture were blown into the air and landed here. Turks call this mountain Büyük Ağri Dağ.

In 1969 the expedition shown in this photograph set out to find the ark on Mount Ararat. So far, though, the ark, if it still exists, has eluded modern explorers.

In 1906 and 1908 George Hagopian, who pastured sheep and goats in the alpine valleys, sighted remains of what he came to believe was Noah's ark. Illustrator Elfred Lee painted these two illustrations based on Hagopian's descriptions.

# THE LORD MAKES ALL THINGS

The biblical teaching about Creation does not just appear in the book of Genesis and its depiction of how the world began. We find it throughout Scripture. And it involves far more than just the truth that God brought physical matter and life into existence.

The Genesis account of the Lord's creative activity stands in sharp contrast to the beliefs of the rest of the nations in the ancient Near East. First, other nations believed that the gods themselves had not always existed. Even they had had a beginning. One god would spontaneously spring into being, and then he would make the other deities in some manner or other. The first god would be the result of the outworking of natural laws inherent in the very fabric of the universe it-

self. The cosmos had always been preprogrammed to create gods for itself. In some ways the concept reminds us of modern evolutionary theories, which suggest that life came into being because of natural physical and chemical laws.

The Mesopotamian gods, once they came into existence, struggled with each other for control. The biblical account has the creation of human beings as the goal of God's creative work. But the Mesopotamian gods created the earth and human beings as an accidental by-product of that conflict. One ancient account portrays the higher gods making human beings so that they could do the work that the lesser gods refused to perform. Otherwise, the focus is on the struggles among the gods themselves.

The ancient Egyptians also regarded the origin of the earth and of its life as the inevitable results of the operation of natural laws. Once the first god came into existence, he made the other deities and everything else through a variety of means. The god named Ptah, who was worshipped particularly in the ancient city of Memphis, spoke everything into being. But the god himself came into being only because of the working of laws already existing in the cosmos. And Ptah did not really create anything through his own power—he just activated something already waiting to be brought into existence. For example, when he said the word "tree," the expression had a tree programmed into it, like cosmic DNA or digital code. Saying "tree" started the process that would form an actual physical tree. Ptah was not creating through his own powers. He was only triggering that which was predetermined to be. Nor was Ptah eternal, as the God of the Bible claimed to be (Psalm 90:1, 2). In fact, the Egyptians believed that their gods—as well as everything else—would someday cease to exist, and the universe itself would collapse back into the chaos that had existed before creation began. Their gods did not creat the universe—the universe created them. They were no more powerful than the universe itself, and thus did not really control it.

The Bible, however, depicts God as standing outside and above all creation. He is not just some natural law at work. Also, the Lord creates through His own power. He is not triggering some latent cosmic law that automatically makes something spring into existence. The ancient pagans saw their gods as merely manifestations of some natural phenomena. For example, Baal was god of storms and fertility, and Ra was one of many Egyptian gods who were different forms of the sun. But Scripture continually declares that God is not part of any force of nature—He is the one who made nature in the first place. The natural world is not God—it is His handiwork, and He is totally separate from it.

The Lord not only created the physical universe and its life forms. Scripture presents Him as still making something else—history. He is involved in the events that take place in His physical creation. Scripture is most interested in this aspect of His creatorship.

God made the world and the beings living in it. Humanity rebelled against Him. But He did not reject His creation because it fell. He works to restore it. His deliverance of His people is as much a demonstration of His creative power as was speaking the earth into existence. The Lord saves His fallen creation through redemptive acts—what some call salvation history. The power that first created the world and human beings

Baal was the personification of fertility and god of stoms and thunder.

This statue of Baal probably once held a lightning bolt.

The power that God used to "stretch out" the heavens and bring stars into existence He also uses to guide the events of our lives.

the heavens, but also creates what happens below them. He can shape the future of nations, such as Assyria. "As I have designed, so shall it be; and as I have planned, so shall it come to pass" (Isaiah 14:24, NRSV). "For the Lord of hosts has planned, and who will annul it? His hand is stretched out, and who will turn it back?" (verse 27, NRSV). Just as He brought the world into being through His power, in the same way He makes human history. "I work and who can hinder it?" (Isaiah 43:13, NRSV).

That does not mean that God predestines everything that happens. He does not select what flavor of ice cream we will like, or determine when and where we will take our vacation. The Lord gives us great freedom of choice, including whether we will accept Him as our God or not. Rather, He focuses on a specific kind of history—He creates the events that will redeem His people. We see that at work in His calling of Cyrus, the Persian ruler, to do great things for God's people after they had been in exile.

When Scripture

God now uses to re-create that creation. For the Bible writers, the ability to create distinguishes between the true God and all false ones.

Bible writers often pointed to His creative power as the proof that He is truly God and not an idol like those worshipped by the pagans. Idols needed someone else to bring them into existence (Isaiah 40:18-20; 44:9-20). But the God of Israel can create—both material things and the events that involve them. The prophet Isaiah declares that God not only stretches out the heavens but blocks the ambitions of human leaders (Isaiah 40:22, 23). Here God links His creative powers with His ability to control political and other historical events. Isaiah goes on to say that "the Lord is the everlasting God, the Creator of the ends of the earth" (verse 28, NRSV).

Thus God not only creates ("stretches out")

These kittens may look alike, but God made each one of them with individual personalities.

first introduces Cyrus in Isaiah 41:2, God asks, "Who has roused a victor from the east, summoned him to his service?" (NRSV). The answer is that it is the Lord's doing. Cyrus will accomplish his mission only through God's power. God makes it happen as He grasps the Persian leader's hand and enables him to conquer other nations (Isaiah 45:1). The Creator goes ahead of him to overcome obstacles so that Cyrus can bring to pass what God wants him to do for Israel (verses 2-4). The Lord arms Cyrus (verse 5) and sets in motion forces that will allow the Persian to fulfill the divine plan. The Lord can do this, Isaiah says, because He is the only God, the Creator who establishes light and darkness and everything else (verses 6, 7). He will arouse Cyrus "in righteousness, and . . . will make all his paths straight" (verse 13, NRSV), because He is the one "who created the heavens (he is God!), who formed the earth and made it. . . . I am the Lord, and there is no other" (verse 18, NRSV).

## SAFE IN THE CREATOR'S HANDS

The fact that God is Creator should comfort us as we struggle with the difficulties and mysteries of life. The power to create enables Him to overcome whatever may happen to His people. Job discovered this as he endured unexplainable suffering and tragedy. Unknown to him, Satan had attacked him and his family (Job 1; 2). Neither Job nor his friends could understand what was happening to him, and he pleaded with God for Him to explain the cause for his suffering. God finally appeared to Job, but He did not reveal the reasons behind what the patriarch

*We see God's control of the universe not only in the stars but also in the beating of the wings and heart of the tiny hummingbird.*

was going through. Instead, the Lord pointed to His creative power, asking Job if he could control creation as God Himself does (Job 38-41), including the powerful creatures Behemoth and Leviathan (Job 40:15–41:11). But God can. And Job must trust the Lord to use that same creative power to control the evil and immorality in the world. The fact that God is Creator assures His people that they will be safe in His hands and that He will be able to redeem them.

God accomplishes salvation through historical events, including those of His people's individual lives. The power that created stars and planets and all kinds of living organisms can also produce conversion and peace and transformation in each person who turns to Him. Thus Creation guarantees salvation.

The New Testament applies the role and power of creatorship to Jesus (John 1:1-3; 1 Corinthians 8:6; Colossians 1:16; Hebrews 1:2). As Creator, Jesus would have the power to redeem and re-create all those who love Him. He would create the greatest historical event of all—His death on the cross. According to the book of Revelation, a divine proclamation will call upon all humanity in the last days to "fear God and give him glory, for the hour of his judgment has come; and worship him who made heaven and earth, the sea and the springs of water" (Revelation 14:7, NRSV). God's people will clearly recognize His role in creating the events that lead to their salvation.

# BIBLE GLOSSARY/DICTIONARY

Here is a list of the biblical people and places mentioned in this book. The glossary not only gives information about each person and place, but also provides two guides that use easy-to-understand pronunciation apparatus. When a syllable is given in all CAPITAL letters, that is the syllable you put the stress on.

The first pronunciation offered is how most people who speak American English say the name. The second pronunciation is truly special. It tells you how to pronounce the name in Hebrew, Egyptian, Persian, Babylonian, Aramaic, or Greek. We give special thanks to Leona G. Running, expert in ancient Near Eastern languages, for preparing the pronunciation guides.

Have fun reading about these fascinating people and places of long ago. And enjoy the edge you'll have when it comes to biblical trivia, because you will be able to pronounce those tongue-twisting names just as they were spoken in the ancient Near East.

**ABEL**—*American English pronunciation: AY-bell. Hebrew pronunciation: ah-VAIL.* The second child born to Adam and Eve. The name in Hebrew means "breath" or "vapor," which may refer to the shortness of his life. In the Akkadian language *aplu* meant "son" or "heir." Abel cared for sheep—the first shepherd. God accepted Abel's sacrifice but rejected Cain's. Why? We do not know for sure. Maybe Cain offered the wrong kind of sacrifice. Perhaps Abel's faith (see Hebrews 11:4) made the offering better.

Abel

**ADAM**—*American English pronunciation: ADD-em. Hebrew pronunciation: ah-DAHM.* The first person created by God in His own image (on the sixth day) in the Genesis Creation story. In Hebrew it can be translated "ruddy" or "clay" as well as "human being." (The same root word in other northwest Semitic languages—Ugaritic and Phoenician—also refers to human beings.) According to the account in Genesis 2, God sculpted the first human being from clay—dirt—and breathed life into him (verse 7). The Hebrew word—even in the Genesis Creation story—has three meanings: (a) human beings in a generic sense, regardless of the person's sex (see Genesis 1:26, 27); (b) the first male human being and has the definite article with it—*"the* man" (Genesis 2:7-25; Genesis 3); and (c) a proper noun—Adam, with no definite article (Genesis 4:1). Adam lived for an unspecified time in the Garden of Eden, which he was supposed to take care of. After he and Eve sinned, God made them leave the garden. Adam died when he was 930 years old.

Adam

**ARARAT**—*American English pronunciation: AIR-a-rat. Hebrew pronunciation: uh-rah-RAHT.* The country (called Urartu in Assyrian) where Noah's ark settled among the mountains as the floodwaters went down. The name can be loosely translated as "mountainous country." It was approximately the size of Kansas. No particular summit is mentioned in the Bible. Several peaks have been traditionally identified as "Mount Ararat," a modern term. One of these, called Masis by today's Armenians, has two peaks (the highest towers 16,945 feet) and lies about midway between the Black Sea and the Caspian Sea. The region is now located in parts of Iran, Iraq, Turkey, and Armenia.

**BABEL**—*American English pronunciation: BAY-bel. Hebrew pronunciation: bah-VEL. Babylonian pronunciation: bahb-EEL-ee.* Babel is a Babylonian word that means "gate of god," but the Hebrew people, who loved to play on words, said it meant "confusion," because it sounded

cherubim

faintly like the Hebrew verb *balal,* which meant "to confuse." Babel was a very old city, and was ruled by Nimrod. It was here on the plain of Shinar that the Tower of Babel was constructed by the post-Flood society, and it was here that God confused human language. The Mesopotamians built many such towers, which we call ziggurats. These structures were a kind of stepped temple of seven stages and could reach heights of more than 300 feet. At the very top, worshippers encountered their deity, such as Marduk.

**CAIN**—*American English pronunciation: CANE. Hebrew pronunciation: KA-yin.* The Old Testament reports on a man and town by the name of Cain. The proper noun means either "worker in metal" or "someone acquired." As recorded in Scripture, Cain—the person—has the distinction of being the first human being born. He was the older brother of Abel. Cain was a farmer and sacrificed to God. However, God did not find his sacrifice pleasing. Angry (and perhaps jealous), Cain became the first

murderer on record; he killed his own brother. The town is sometimes spelled Kain. It was situated in the hills of Judah, some three miles southeast of Hebron.

**CHERUBIM**—*American English pronunciation: CHAIR-ub(im). Hebrew pronunciation: ke-ROOV/ke-roo-VEEM.* These two Hebrew words appear 92 times in the Old Testament. Often considered by many Christians as a class of angelic beings, the descriptive hints that we find in the Bible would lead us to conclude that they are "imaginative constructs" of some sort. Cherubim (the plural form of cherub—not cherubs) appears in conjunction with the sanctuary, Temple, and God's personal presence. They are described as amalgamated or hybrid beings, which is why scholars refer to them as "unnatural beings" or "fanciful composite beings." Cherubim were associated with God's throne and appear to function as moving Him or moving with Him. The one common feature of cherubim in the Old Testament is that they had wings. Otherwise, their appearance is not consistent in all descriptions of them. The cherubim that hover over the ark of the covenant in the Mosaic sanctuary appear to have a single face. However, Ezekiel describes them in one place as having two faces and in another as having four faces—human, bovine, leonine, and aquiline. Sometimes they have two legs; sometimes four. These biblical descriptions bear a striking resemblance to the statues of other hybrid creatures discovered by archaeologists in the ancient Near East, especially in Assyria.

**EDEN**—*American English pronunciation: EE-den. Hebrew pronunciation: AϒY-den.* The Hebrew place name Eden probably means either "steppe" or "delight." It was the name of the plain on which God planted a luxurious garden for Adam and Eve to live in. According to Genesis, two special trees grew in Eden. One was the tree of life; the other was the tree of the knowledge of good and evil. God gave Adam and Eve only one commandment (not 10): Do not eat the fruit growing on the tree of the knowledge

of good and evil. They did, thus rebelling against God. Much speculation has gone into identifying Eden and its garden. No one knows for sure where it was situated, although some scholars think it was somewhere in Mesopotamia—maybe north in Armenia or south in Babylonia. Much later in the Old Testament the Garden of Eden seems to be identical with the Garden of God and the Garden of Yahweh. An ancient Sumerian story talks about Dilmun. It was a place in which illness, old age, and death were unknown. That sounds very much like the paradise of Eden described in the book of Genesis, doesn't it?

**ENOCH**—*American English pronunciation: EE-nok. Hebrew pronunciation: ha-NOHK.* Two men and one city in the Old Testament bore the name Enoch, which means "dedicated one." He was the "seventh from Adam" and is said to have "walked with God" after his wife gave birth to Methuselah. Scholars are not sure how to understand the Hebrew behind the expression "walked with God," because it has the definite article and uses the plural form of

Eden

God, which can be translated "walked with the gods" (in the Hebrew Bible angels were sometimes designated by the Hebrew word *elohim*). When Enoch was 365 years old, God translated him—took him alive to heaven.

**EVE**—*American English pronunciation: EEV. Hebrew pronunciation: ha-WAH.* The meaning of the word is unclear, but it may have overtones meaning "ancestress" or "living one" or "one who gives birth." The Hebrew pronunciation of her name sounds like the word for "life," although the two Hebrew words derive from different roots. Some linguists have noted that an old Aramaic word is nearly identical to the Hebrew root, and this archaic Aramaic word means "snake" or "serpent." Whether or not this is purely coincidental remains to be determined. As most people know, Eve was tempted by a serpent in the Garden of Eden. According to the Genesis account of Creation, God made Eve from one of Adam's ribs. Having been created prior to Eve, Adam appeared lonely. God decided that one human being alone in the Garden of Eden was "not good." So He put Adam to sleep and fashioned the first woman from a rib. When the first man awoke from his deep sleep and saw the first woman, he burst into song about her. Immediately Adam named her *Ishshah*, "woman," but after the Fall renamed her Eve. The Bible says that she was a "helper fit for" Adam. Some interpreters have decided this meant that Eve was in some way to be subordinate to Adam. However, the way the word "helper" is used in the Hebrew Bible, it does not connote subordination. It was even used to describe God, the Helper of the Hebrew people.

**HAM**—*American English pronunciation: HAM. Hebrew pronunciation: HAHM.* This name of one of Noah's three sons probably means "hot." According to the biblical text of Genesis, Ham was born sometime after Noah was 500 years old. When Noah became drunk from too much wine after the Flood, Ham did not behave properly in honoring his father. In fact, evidence from certain documents found

Eve

in the ancient city of Ugarit leads us to believe that Ham's gazing upon Noah's nakedness (exactly what happened is open to speculation) was likely considered a criminal act. Consequently Noah cursed, not Ham, but his son Canaan. This shifting of the curse has puzzled interpreters. Some think they see evidence that Canaan was actually not Ham's own son but a fourth son of Noah—and that somehow the names got confused in the process of transmission. Such an approach, of course, flies in the face of what the biblical text actually says. The African and Arabian Cushites were descendants of Ham. In some biblical poetry the term *Ham* refers to the country of Egypt. Ham's sons are listed as Cush (Ethiopia), Egypt, Put (Libya), and Canaan— all ancestors of ancient nations. It is a mistake to refer to the "curse of Ham" as the justification for the enslavement of people of Negroid descent. The biblical text is clear that Noah cursed Canaan, the ancestor of the Hebrew people's enemy (Canaanites) par excellence and that Ham's gazing upon Noah's nakedness was likely considered a criminal act.

Japheth

**JAPHETH**—*American English pronunciation: JAY-feth. Hebrew pronunciation: YEH-feth.* The name may mean "beauty" or "let him make wide" or "may he have space." The meaning is speculative and debated among linguists. Japheth was born after Noah was 500 years old. Whether Japheth was Noah's youngest or oldest son depends on how one understands the biblical data. We know little about him except that he and his brother Shem treated Noah with dignity when Ham reported his

drunken condition. Japheth, with his seven sons, was the progenitor of the Japhethites, a group of Indo-European peoples that included the Medes, Ionians, and several nations living in what was later called Asia Minor and southern Russia.

**LUCIFER**—*American English pronunciation: LOO-sif-er. (Not in Bible.)* This proper name is the Latin equivalent ("light bearer") of the Hebrew *hêlel*, which means "shining one" or "to be brilliant." Isaiah 14:12 uses the terminology in reference to a special being, whom Isaiah called "son of the morning," which was a common way of referring to the planet Venus when it was the "morning star." Although Isaiah also identifies this individual as the "king of Babylon," many Christians believe this biblical passage refers to Satan before he became God's enemy but was an angel of light. This identification, which is supported by some of the Church Fathers but is not explicit in Scripture, results from equating Jesus' words "I saw Satan fall like lightning from heaven" (Luke 10:18) with Isaiah 14.

Methuselah

**METHUSELAH**—*American English pronunciation: meh-THOO-ze-lah. Hebrew pronunciation: me-thoo-SHELL-akh.* This name probably means either "man of the javelin" or "worshipper of Selah," a strange name that Enoch and his wife bestowed upon their son. It could refer to Šalaḥ, god of the infernal river, but linguists have found no other personal names that incorporated this ancient pagan deity's name. Methuselah was born when Enoch was 65 years old. According to the biblical genealogies, Methuselah lived to be 969 years old, the oldest living person ever, dying when Noah was 600 years old. Methuselah was the father of Lamech (Genesis 5:25) and Noah's grandfather. According to Genesis 4:18, the name of Lamech's father was Methushael. It is probable that Genesis gives alternative spellings for the name of the same individual. In this second instance, the *shael* ending may come from the term *sheol*, which became the Hebrew term for the abode of the dead or grave but also appears to have been early on the name of deity.

**MOSES**—*American English pronunciation: MOH-zez. Hebrew pronunciation: moh-SHEH.* The name in Hebrew means "one drawn out," but it could well have been a shortened Egyptian form that ended the names of several pharaohs—Ahmose, Ramose, and Thutmose, for example, which meant something like "child of." Since Pharaoh's daughter rescued Moses from the Nile River, known as the god Hapi, it may have been that she called him Hapimose. The Egyptians often shortened these names to just "Mose." It is possible that somewhere along the line the Hebrew people forgot that Moses' name was originally Egyptian. Scholars speculate that they thus thought his name was thoroughly Hebrew (Canaanite) in character and came from the Hebrew root meaning "drawn out." Moses' first years—until weaning—were with his own parents. But overall his first 40 years were in the Egyptian court. The next 40 years he spent in exile in Midian, where he married Zipporah, the daughter of Jethro (also known as Reuel). While Moses was in the wilderness tending a flock of sheep, God called him at the burning bush and commissioned him to return to Egypt so he could lead the Israelites from Egypt to the Promised Land. It was during the exodus from Egypt that Moses received from God the law that the Hebrew people cherished. Because Moses disobeyed God by hitting a rock for water rather than speaking to it, he died without having the privilege of entering Canaan. He was the son of Amram and Jochebed, and the brother of Miriam and Aaron. (Aaron was 3 years older than Moses.)

**NOAH**—*American English pronunciation: NOH-ah. Hebrew pronunciation: NOH-akh.* The Old Testament mentions two people who had the name Noah—one a male and the other a female. The name means "rest." The Noah in *101 Favorite Bible Stories* is the one whom God asked to build the ark. The boat Noah built was 450 feet long, 75 feet wide, and 45 feet high. (The *Mayflower* was 90 feet long. The *Queen Mary* is 1,109.5 feet long. The *Titanic* was 800 feet in length.) According to the book of Genesis, Noah, through his sons and daughters-in-law who survived the Flood, became the progenitor of the human race. When God first told Noah about the forthcoming flood, this son of Lamech was about 480 years old. Noah was about 600 years old when the Flood came, and he died at the age of 950 years. He is the first recorded person to have planted a vineyard.

Noah

Sabbath

**SABBATH**—*American English pronunciation: SAB-bath. Hebrew pronunciation: shab-BAHT.* The Hebrew word means "cessation" or "rest." The Sabbath is the seventh day of the week—modern Saturday. This was the day on which the Hebrew people worshipped their God as they celebrated Creation week and the exodus from Egypt. It was regarded as a sign of God's covenant with them. Not only were the Hebrew people themselves to rest on the Sabbath, but their animals and servants were also to take part in this weekly day of rest. According to the Gospel accounts, Jesus Himself worshipped on the Sabbath—on Saturday. And the evidence in the rest of the New Testament indicates that the early Christian church continued that practice.

**SATAN**—*American English pronunciation: SAY-tan. Hebrew pronunciation: sah-TAHN. Greek pronunciation: sah'tah-NAHS.* The word means "accuser," sometimes with the connotation of "adversary." The Hebrew word appears in the Bible as a verb as well as a noun.

The verb has nuances that range from "accuse" to "slander." The noun could refer to human beings as well as to a celestial being. The first use of the noun in connection with a person is David's being called "satan" (1 Samuel 29:4). Abishai and his officials, sons of Zeruíah, were called "satans" by David (2 Samuel 19:18-22). Solomon later says that he no longer had any "satans" (military enemies) and so was ready to begin constructing the Temple (1 Kings 5:4, 18). Later, however, King Hadad (1 Kings 11:14) and King Rezon (verses 23, 25) were said to be Solomon's "satans." As to the supernatural or celestial "satan," the noun seems originally to have referred to a position or function and so was used with the definite article in Hebrew: *ha satan*—the accuser. Numbers 22:22, 23 does not use the definite article but identifies the angel of YHWH as "a satan." Also in the last Old Testament book to be written the definite article is missing, which can be translated "an adversary" or "Satan," the personal name of an individual. (See 1 Chronicles 21:1.) In the other two uses of the term (Job 1; 2 and Zechariah 3:1, 2), "the satan" is a functionary in God's court and not considered God's enemy. As the adversary, it was his job to accuse people before God and thereby test their loyalty. In the New Testament the word serves as the devil's proper name—the being who heads up the demonic forces of evil. Some rabbis said that the serpent that tempted Eve in the Garden of Eden was really Satan, a person (*the* person) who personified evil and led the demonic hordes. Satan, the person, is mentioned 35 times in the New Testament. Despite his evil intentions, Satan does not have unlimited power. God will ultimately triumph over him, casting him in the lake of fire described in Revelation 20:10.

**SHEM**—*American English pronunciation: SHEM. Hebrew pronunciation: SHAYM.* The word means "name" or "renown." Shem was the son of Noah, perhaps his middle son, though not all biblical scholars agree on this. Shem had five sons: Elam, Asshur, Arpachshad, Lud, and Aram. He was the progenitor of the Semite people, including the Babylonians, Assyrians, Aramaeans, Arabs, and Israelites. Shem was born 98 years before the Flood, when Noah was 502 years old. Some Jewish traditions indicate that Shem was a priest, and some (a bit far-fetched, to be sure) identified him with Melchizedek. He is, according to some traditions, the founder of the first school. Luke's genealogy of Jesus lists Shem as one of His forefathers. Shem died when he was 600 years old.

**SHINAR (place)**—*American English pronunciation: SHY-nar. Hebrew pronunciation: shin-AHR.* Shinar was another biblical name for Babylonia. The Tower of Babel was erected on the plain of Shinar. One of the kings of Shinar, Amraphel, made war with the king of Sodom (Genesis 14:1, 2) and ended up capturing Lot and his family. Abraham put together a posse and recaptured his nephew and the booty taken from the cities near the Dead Sea. The name may come from the cuneiform term *Samharû,* which was a Kassite tribe that lived in the region.

Shem and his wife

# RUTH REDDING BRAND

Ruth Redding Brand, assistant professor of English at Atlantic Union College in Massachusetts, has written the main stories in this book. Bible stories have fascinated her from the time she was a child. When the Review and Herald Publishing Association invited her to explore the Holy Land with the late Siegfried Horn, a world-renowned archaeologist and eminently knowledgeable tour guide, she eagerly accepted. That experience (along with a lot of research) gave her access to an authenticity of detail that makes the narratives in the Family Bible Story books live and breathe.

Brand was raised on a dairy farm in Maine and grew up milking cows, haying, riding hefty work-

FINKLE PHOTOGRAPHY

horses, and pulling weeds in acres of corn and cucumbers. As an adult she has taught elementary school and junior high as well as college. Since earning her Master's degree in English, she has taught English at Fitchburg State College and Atlantic Union College.

She lives in Lancaster, Massachusetts, with her husband, Bob, and pampered cat, Sky. She is blessed with two adult children, Jeffrey and Heidi, and their respective spouses, Krista (Motschiedler) and Troy Clark. Brand loves to read, play word games, walk on the beach, and swim, but she'll drop any of these activities in a heartbeat to spend time with her granddaughter, little Miss Emma Mae Clark!

# LINDA PORTER CARLYLE

Linda Porter Carlyle, who wrote the Bible bedtime stories for this book, says, "I love the poetry and the music of words. I especially take pleasure in writing read-aloud stories for the very young."

Carlyle lives with her husband, two beautiful daughters, one dog, three cats, and two rabbits on a quiet dead-end, tree-lined street. She homeschools her children, Sarah and Abby.

Among her favorite things are paper and pencils and pens. She also savors the quietness of a library,

the smell of books, the feel of their pages, and the way the words look printed there.

Linda Porter Carlyle hopes that parents and children will be able to cuddle close to each other and enjoy—again and again—these Bible bedtime stories together. These stories also provide good exercises for beginning readers.

# LEONA GLIDDEN RUNNING

Even as a little girl, Leona Glidden Running found foreign languages fascinating. In high school she learned Spanish from an older student who taught her during lunchtime. In college she majored in French and minored in German, which she later taught at the high school level.

For four years Running worked for the Voice of Prophecy, a well-known religious radiobroadcast originating from California, where she typed scripts in Spanish and Portuguese. During that time her husband, Leif (Bud) Running, died. She felt as though she were in a tunnel for eight years. Then she fell seriously ill, and when she recovered, Running attended seminary, where she learned biblical Greek and Hebrew. From there she began teaching seminary classes in biblical languages while she worked on a doctorate in Semitic languages at Johns Hopkins University.

For many years Running taught ancient languages at Andrews University in Michigan. Even after her retirement she taught Egyptian hieroglyphics, Assyrian/Babylonian cuneiform, and ancient Syriac for 21 more years. Today Running enjoys total retirement from the classroom. She encourages young people with these words: "Find your gift, develop it, and let God use it!"

Leona Glidden Running reviewed for accuracy the stories in the Family Bible Story series. She also prepared the pronunciation guide at the end of this book.

# HEATHER GROVET

Heather Grovet lives in Alberta, Canada, with her husband, Doug. They have two daughters, Danelle and Kaitlin.

Grovet's hobbies include training and showing horses (she's been involved with horses since she was 10 years old), reading, and . . . talking! As you can tell from the Bible bedtime stories that she wrote for this book, writing is another of her hobbies. In fact, she has had many books published. Among these books are *Prince: the Persnickety Pony; Petunia the Ugly Pug; Marvelous Mark and His No-good Dog; and What's Wrong With Rusty?*

Grovet is happiest when she is outside on a beautiful summer day, riding her horse. She's least happy when she has to do sewing and ironing or must take a long trip in the car.

She says that the one word that best describes her is *determined*. She writes, "God has put a lot of time into helping me with my patience, but I still need to improve. Also, I need to be careful not to get so busy that I forget to keep Him first."

Grovet advises young people: "God loves you even when you don't feel very lovable. Don't ever forget that."

# RAOUL VITALE

Starting at the age of 3, Raoul Vitale began drawing, using Bible stories for ideas. There he found sufficient exciting accounts to last a lifetime!

After graduating high school, he accepted employment as an artist/designer for a local stained glass studio, where he worked for 25 years. During his spare time Vitale, who had no formal art training, experimented with different techniques, learning by trial and error. During this period he occasionally illustrated for local magazines and produced some murals.

In 1998 Vitale decided to illustrate full-time and was also able to work with a variety of concept artists developing collectibles and creating original oil paintings. Soon he was preparing illustrations for magazines and books.

Vitale says of the Bible, "It's so rich in imagery, culture, history, and scope that it's difficult to do justice to the stories in my illustrations. How do you illustrate the creation of a universe that God spoke into existence? I'm very grateful to be able to do what I love and make a living at it! God has opened many doors."

He and his wife, Christine, live in Canton, Ohio, with their son Santino. They enjoy helping Santino with his dream of preparing stop-motion animation. They also delight in spending time with their church family as well as serving as Awana leaders for boys and girls between the ages 8 and 12.

The development of each of the pieces of artwork in this book goes through a certain process. Raoul Vitale went through various rough sketches as he refined this image of Eve giving Adam the forbidden fruit. All of his work is submitted to an oversight committee that reviews them and makes suggestions for possible improvements.

Here we see an electronic composite of his tight sketch and the final rendering.

# DARREL TANK

One of Darrel Tank's earliest memories of art is drawing pictures with his mother. She encouraged his creativity, which was apparent even when he was a very small child. While growing up, he often spent his afternoons at the publishing house where his father was the head photographer. The work of the illustrators there particularly fascinated him, and he began to dream of pursuing a career in art.

Tank was able to accomplish that dream in the late seventies and has exhibited and received honors at numerous art shows with his sensitive approach to portraiture. His photo-realistic style shows remarkable attention to fine detail and captures the emotion of the moment.

Tank and his wife, Denise, have four children and 12 grandchildren. They live in Garden Valley, Idaho, up in the mountains where they have snow for three to four months of the year. He writes, "We are sur-rounded by meadows, forests of pines and firs, and groves of aspens. There's a tremendous amount of wildlife, including herds of elk and deer, foxes, bears, mountain lions, wild turkeys, bald eagles, raccoons, Canada geese, and so much more."

The Tanks have an "extremely smart" yellow Labrador retriever named Chamois. She knows many tricks and loves to perform them for visitors. They also have two cats. One is 13 years old and is named Sienna, because of her color. The other is a pure white, long-haired cat.

Tank's repertoire includes black-and-white pencil renderings, color pencil, gouache, airbrush paintings, and computer illustrations, which have appeared in more than 400 books, magazines, advertising, and prints.

Darrel Tank goes through many steps before completing his pencil illustrations. He has to select models and have them photographed in their specific poses. He frequently has biblical attire specially made for his models, which helps him make the image look more realistic.

The image to the left is an electronic composite of Darrel's initial sketch and the finished image.

# ACKNOWLEDGMENTS

Where does one begin? So many individuals have helped in the construction of this unique book. We owe all a great debt of gratitude for the time and effort they invested to make the book a reality. Perhaps we can talk in categories of influence.

## RESEARCH

*Gail Hunt,* who had the first vision of a multilayer book and then conducted 11 focus groups around the United States

*Richard W. Coffen,* who brainstormed with Mr. Hunt and became director of the project

*Gerald Wheeler,* who as a Bible lover and book editor embraced the concept

*Patricia Fritz,* who spent many hours coordinating myriads of details

*Bob Haddock and Associates,* who helped with early marketing plans

The **many men and women and boys and girls** who shared their valuable ideas at the focus groups

## ADMINISTRATION

*Harold F. Otis, Jr.,* president who caught the vision immediately

*Robert S. Smith,* president who insisted on moving ahead after years of delay

*Hepsiba S. Singh,* treasurer who offered the financial support needed

*Mark B. Thomas,* vice president of the Book Division, who helped facilitate development and chaired our oversight committee

*Jeannette Johnson,* acquisitions editor, who kept minutes for the oversight committtee

*Trent Truman,* art coordinator, who prepared the layout and design and worked with the talented illustrators who provided such amazing artwork

## WRITERS

*Ruth Redding Brand,* who researched and wrote the main stories in this series

*Linda Porter Carlyle and Heather Grovet,* who wrote the Bible bedtime stories

*Leona Glidden Running,* who prepared the pronunciation guide in the glossary/Bible dictionary

*Richard W. Coffen and Gerald Wheeler,* who wrote the DID YOU KNOW? sections

*Constance Clark Gane,* who prepared the time lines

## ILLUSTRATIVE ENDEAVORS

Raoul Vitale     Darrel Tank

## YOUNG READERS

| | | | | |
|---|---|---|---|---|
| Benjamin Baker | Nathan Blake | Annalise Harvey | Katrina Pepper | Bradley Thomas |
| David Baker | Coramina Cogan | Alyssa Harvey | Lisa Sayler | Jeremy Tooley |
| Emily Barr | Raeven Cogan | Garrick Herr | Emily Shockey | Tara Van Hyning |
| Jacob Barr | Rande Colburn | Alicia O'Connor | Katie Shockey | Kim Wasenmiller |
| Carin Bartlett | Zoë Rose Fritz | Jeremy Pepper | Jonathan Singh | Tompaul Wheeler |
| Caitlyn Bartlett | Jennifer Hanson | Jessica Pepper | Kaitlyn Singh | Megan Williams |

## SCHOLARLY INPUT

| | | | |
|---|---|---|---|
| *Douglas Clark* | *Siegfried Horn* | *Pedrito Maynard-Reid* | *Warren Trenchard* |
| *Larry Herr* | *John R. Jones* | *Leona Glidden Running* | *S. Douglas Waterhouse* |
| *Lawrence T. Geraty* | *Sakae Kubo* | *Ronald Springett* | *Randall Younker* |

## LITERARY INPUT

*Denise Herr,* college English teacher     *Shelley Pocha,* college student of Ms. Herr

*Kelly Bird,* college student of Ms. Herr     *Sherry Rusk,* college student of Ms. Herr

*Orval Driskel,* marketer     *Sandy Robinson,* marketer

*Tracy Fry,* college student of Ms. Herr     *Sheri Rusk,* college student of Ms. Herr

*Susan Harvey,* marketer     *Doug Sayles,* marketer

*Eugene Lincoln,* editor     *Gerald Wheeler,* editor

*Donna Martens,* college student of Ms. Herr     *Penny Wheeler,* editor

*Ray Woolsey,* editor

## EDITORIAL HELP

*Eugene Lincoln,* who helped edit     *James Cavil,* copy editor

and copyedit early versions     *Jocelyn Fay,* copy editor

*Delma Miller,* copy editor

## RESOURCE COORDINATOR

*Tompaul Wheeler*